Beautifully Broken

Memoirs From Trauma to Triumph

By Kar'Michay Pope

Kar'Michay Pope

First Edition
ISBN: 979-8-218-73488-6
Printed in the United States of America
Cover design by Karmel Pope
Edited by Karmel Pope

This is a work of nonfiction. Some names and identifying details may have been changed to protect the privacy of individuals.

Acknowledgments

Writing this book has been one of the most vulnerable and healing journeys of my life. I could not have done it alone.

First and foremost, I thank God for being my constant source of strength, healing, and hope. When I felt like I could not go on, You carried me. This book is a testimony to Your grace in the darkest places.

To my mom and dad, sister, family, and friends who have stood beside me, encouraged me, and reminded me of my worth when I forgot it myself, thank you. Your love has been a light through every shadow.

To the mentors, counselors, and spiritual guides who poured into my healing journey, your wisdom and compassion helped me piece together what felt irreparably broken. I am forever grateful for your presence and guidance.

To the survivors, those I have met and those I have not yet, you are my inspiration. Your courage to keep going, to fight for healing, and to rise despite it all is what gave me the strength to share my story. This book is for you.

And to every person who reads these pages: thank you. Thank you for opening your heart to mine. May you find in these words a mirror of your own resilience, and may you remember that even in brokenness, there is beauty.

With all my heart,
Kar'Michay Pope

Kar'Michay Pope

Table of Contents

Preface...6
Introduction 8
Welcome Aboard, My Journey Called Life "Beautifully
Broken" 11

The Egg: The Beginning / Hope In The Hidden / Early Wounds
(My innocence didn't save me)
Story 1: Fly Me To The Moon 17
Story 2: A Pony Kind Of Christmas................................24
Story 3: The Mystery Man...29
Story 4: Angel Of My Dreams 33
Story 5: Back To The Basics?..36
Story 6: A Southern Grandmother 42
Story 7: The Spiritual One...45
Story 8: A Mystery No More...50

The Caterpillar: Growth / Struggle / Learning
(Getting through what should have killed me)
Story 9: Is God Real? 57
Story 10: Shattered Trust 61
Story 11: The Year Of Completion 65
Story 12: What Goes Up Must Come Down....................68
Story 13: The Fight 72
Story 14: Poolside 75
Story 15: A Dish Or Two..79
Story 16: Numb..82
Story 17: The Thief In The Night.....................................88
Story 18: Lost And Alone 93
Story 19: Invisible 99
Story 20: The New Normal 103

The Chrysalis: Isolation / Breaking / Inner Work
(The breaking that builds you)

Story 21: Take Me To The King..110
Story 22: The Perfect Day...113
Story 23: Fresh Start..118
Story 24: What's In A Name (Tpid) 122
Story 25: Jeremiah 129
Story 26: Run 134
Story 27: From Fear To Faith..143
Story 28: In The Club...147
Story 29: A Dream Or A Vision..152

The Butterfly: Freedom / Triumph / New Life
(Flying with scars)

Story 30: Top Of The Ninth Inning 157
Story 31: A Chocolate Adventure...160
Story 32: Winter Games 163
Story 33: A Birthdays To Remember...167
Story 34: Sweet Home Alabama 172
Story 35: Trapped...176
Story 36: I Got Soul 180
Story 37: Over The Ledge 185
Story 38: The Hills That Roll 191
Story 39: Never Forgotten..195
Story 40: From Trauma To Triumph...198

Therapeutic Ways To Release..*204*

Preface

There was a time when I believed my story was too broken to matter and too shattered to be seen, much less shared. But life has taught me that beauty often rises from brokenness, and that some of the most profound triumphs are born from pain.

Beautifully Broken is not just a title; it is the truth of my life. This memoir is a collection of pieces: pieces of sorrow, pain, survival, strength, and healing. Like a butterfly emerging from a cocoon, I have passed through stages of darkness, struggle, and transformation. These stories were written in my trauma and in my triumph, in silence and in finding my voice, in survival and in living fully. They span from age five well into my adult years, sharing moments of confusion, abuse, neglect, and pain while also reflecting on how healing has shaped my perspective along the way.

I wrote this book for the ones who have ever felt lost or alone in their pain, for the ones who have cried in silence, fought battles no one could see, or carried scars like secrets. In other words, I wrote this book for me... and everyone like me. I want you to know healing is possible, even if it may not seem like it today. Wholeness is possible, and your story, just like mine, is not over.

These pages hold truth, vulnerability, pain, and hope. The **Personal Discovery** sections at the end of each story are an offering meant to light the way for you on your own path to healing. My hope is that as you read, my reflection and growth will help you discover your own strength and deposit the courage to keep going within you.

This is not a book written out of anger, and it is not about blaming or pointing fingers. It is about healing, overcoming, and self-discovery. I share my truth in love, and I ask only that you read with compassion.

You are not alone. And you are not beyond repair. You are beautifully broken, and that is where your power begins.

With love and life,
Kar'Michay Pope

Introduction

*B*eautifully *Broken* is not written from a place of having "arrived," and it's not your typical feel-good type of book. Far from it! It is written from the middle of the journey... raw, real, and still unfolding. For as long as I can remember, I have carried pain like a second skin. Trauma was not a single event. It was layered, ongoing, and often hidden beneath a brave face and a quiet voice. In this book, I share graphic, detailed memories of abuse, loss, abandonment, and rejection, as each of these left their mark on my soul. Yet, I also share stories of hope, love, peace, and redemption. I did not wait to write this until I had all the answers. I am writing it now because I finally found the courage to tell the truth aloud, not just for me, but for others like me. For years, I survived. But survival is different from healing. And healing is not a straight path.

Beautifully Broken is my honest account, in the form of short stories, of that not-so-straight path: the breakdowns, the detours, the breakthroughs, and the slow, sacred process of becoming whole. The stories may not follow a perfect chronological order because the book is divided into stages, much like the life of a butterfly. Each stage contains a set of stories that align with that stage's purpose. Trust the flow. Let it meet you where you are. **The Egg** stage represents beginnings. These are stories of firsts in my life, starting with my adoption story. These are the moments before I even realized transformation was possible. These are the seeds of survival. **The Caterpillar** stage is where the future butterfly doesn't yet know it will fly. It crawls through life unprotected. These are stories of oppression, pain, abuse, and hardship. Some contain my most horrid, graphic memories. I understand many readers may find them too difficult to read. But they are my stories, my experiences, my truths. Much of my healing came through writing these stories, and I hope you find healing in the journey as well. **The Chrysalis** stage (also called the cocoon stage) brings stillness, physical safety, and the anticipation of profound change. These are stories of hope amid despair—stories of rescue that prepared me to fly. **The Butterfly** stage is the emergence into something new, something transformed. Most of these stories take place after my escape from the environment of trauma and after my adoption into a new family and life. At the end, I've listed **Therapeutic Ways to Release** trauma and emotional pain. These methods were helpful to me, and I hope they will be helpful to you as well.

Throughout the book, you'll find stories that may be difficult to read. Trust me, this book is for mature audiences only. Some stories may be triggering, and some contain moments of horrific trauma and despair that once felt endlessly hopeless to me. If at any point you feel overwhelmed, pause. Breathe. Maybe visit **Therapeutic Ways to Release** and come back when you are ready. This book is meant to walk with you, not push you. Consider reading it with a trusted counselor or mentor by your side for support. Stories containing graphic content will be labeled, and you may choose to skip them if needed. But please do not stop there. In this book, you will also find stories of hope, redemption, victory, and growth. You will see moments where light broke through the darkness. I understand that not everyone will see these moments the same way I did, and that is okay. I simply ask that you hold space for my truth as I experienced it.

Each story is followed by a **Personal Discovery**, which includes my reflections and lessons learned, followed by questions to guide your own self-reflection and growth. You are invited and encouraged to take your time with each question and write your answers in a journal or workbook. As you answer, I encourage you to dig deep into your own story. Be completely honest. Be open. Give yourself grace through the journey. Who knows… your writings might lead to your own book!

Beautifully Broken is for the ones still walking through the fire. It is for those on a healing journey that feels endless. It is for anyone who has asked, "Will I ever feel whole again?" My answer to you is this: yes, it is absolutely possible. Through my painful and hard journey, I want you to begin thinking about your own journey and remember that you are not alone. Someone out there loves you. Most importantly, it's Jesus… but it's also me. Though I can't heal you or love you or turn things around for you or restore you like He can, I can see you. I can walk with you through this journey. And your journey, however painful, has a purpose. You do not have to be perfect to begin healing. You just need to be willing. I know it hurts. I know that what you've been through is something you may not be able to talk about because of the pain. Know that I SEE YOU. I GET YOU. You are NOT alone.

Welcome Aboard, My Journey Called Life "Beautifully Broken"

I was born in a West Coast city to a mother who was just a baby having a baby, and to a father who wanted nothing to do with me. By the time I was five, I knew what it felt like to be hurt and violated in unimaginable ways. Saying my innocence was taken at a very young age would be an understatement. It was violently snatched away over and over. I understood what it was like not to feel loved, wanted, or accepted, even before I truly understood those words. While most kids were outside playing with friends or inside playing with toys and dolls, I was being passed around to the highest bidder—whoever could give my mom what she wanted, loved, and desired more than me: drugs. Sure, my life wasn't all bad. I had some glimmers of hope shining through here and there. But as I grew up, I quickly realized that my body did not belong to me; it belonged to my mom, and she used it at her disposal to sell to the highest drug dealer's bid.

I was the oldest of my siblings, and I felt that it was my job to protect them from the pain that afflicted me. So, I took it for them. I made sure that their life was as normal as it could possibly be. Our mother was on drugs and would frequently go on what we would call missions. Meaning, she would leave for days or weeks on her drug binges. During these times, it was up to me to make sure my siblings ate and went to school, and it was up to me to make sure the bills got paid and there was food in the house. At a very young age and in a very unsafe environment, I was taking on these responsibilities. So, when she was there, she was selling me for drugs; when she was not there, her "friends" were making me do those same things to pay for the rent and food they were covering. Did I want to be used in this way? Did I want to feel violated all the time? Did I want to experience so much physical and emotional pain? The answer is a resounding NO! Of course not! However, even though they didn't give me a choice, I knew that if I did not give them what they wanted, they would hurt me and not do anything for my siblings or me. I had a sister to protect, and as much as I could help it, they were not about to take her innocence like they took mine.

Of course, the situation with my family caused me to be in and out of foster care. Some might think that this is where the glimmers of light came into my childhood. NO, it was not! Out of all the foster homes I was in, there was only one that treated me like I was truly a valued member of their family. I usually felt like I was the foster child with the note that was written across my forehead that said, "VIOLATE ME!" because that was what continually happened. The glimmers of light in my childhood came from those who took the time to care, to see me for me, and to realize I was hurting and needing help just by looking at the sadness in my eyes. I grew up just wanting to be a normal child, wanting to have the same things that other children had, wanting to go to school and learn. I missed so much school by having to be a parent to my siblings and by moving around so much.

Once I graduated from high school, I was barely surviving, trying to squeeze some sort of semblance of normal life out of the brokenness that my past had left me. The pain I experienced and carried was so great, and throughout my teenage and young adult years, I tried nearly everything besides the drugs I saw my mother taking to ease my pain, including multiple suicide attempts. Then, in an unexpected turn of events, I found myself in unfamiliar territory. I was living in a place of unfamiliarity and uncertainty, having to fully put my trust in things I had never experienced before. I was on the other side of the country, finally safe and free from the bondage that had held me captive for so very long.

The journey was not easy. I fought the very thing I craved, freedom. I wanted to be free, I wanted to be healed, but I did not realize that I was going to have to walk through the pain to get to those outcomes. Healing often hurts first; no one ever tells you that part. Not only did I fight the healing, but I also fought the very people that God had sent to help me through said healing. In the end, I won, and God got the glory; however, it's not over. The journey to complete healing and wholeness is an ongoing thing.

Beautifully Broken simply refers to the idea that although someone has been hurt, wounded, or gone through significant struggles, they can come through those experiences with deeper strength, compassion, wisdom, or authenticity. Growth and healing can come from pain. There is beauty in imperfection and vulnerability. Your "brokenness" can become part of what makes you unique and beautiful. So, welcome aboard my journey called life. Let's jump in together.

Personal Discovery:

I've come to understand that being broken is not the end of my story, but the beginning of a deeper, more authentic one. The cracks in my heart, the battles I've faced, and the broken pieces I've had to gather have not made me less; they've made me real. I am beautifully broken, not despite my pain, but because I allowed the pain to shape me without letting it define me. In my vulnerability, I've found strength. In my healing, I've found purpose. Each scar is a testament to my survival, each flaw, a reflection of my humanity. I am not perfect, but I am whole in a way only those who've rebuilt themselves can understand.

1. What does "beautifully broken" mean to you personally?
2. How can you carry your brokenness with dignity and grace instead of shame?
3. What does wholeness mean to you now? What steps have you taken or can you take to move toward wholeness?
4. What scars, physically, emotionally, or spiritually, have shaped who you are today?

Egg

Psalm 139:13. "For you created my inmost being; you knit me together in my mother's womb."

The Beginning / Hope in the Hidden / Early Wounds

(My innocence didn't save me)

This stage represents beginnings that are fragile or full of potential and often unfold in unexpected ways. Just as an egg holds the mystery of what is to come, these stories reflect important firsts in my life. Some of these firsts are joyful, while others carry pain, yet each one helped shape the foundation of who I am. The Egg stage can be both beautiful and challenging, especially when the beginning of life does not go as planned. In this section, you will find stories from my early childhood as well as my first steps into unfamiliar environments. These are the starting points, the seeds of identity, resilience, and hope, shared in their raw and honest form.

Story 1: Fly Me to the Moon

Four words were never said more beautifully: "You are her parents." I thought, "Wow! I finally have a family! I have parents who actually want me!" But how did we get to these words? It started with an email that was sent that simply stated, "I love your video so much. I'm going to watch it one last time before I take my life." This video was a dance ministry video that I had bought online, but to me, it was everything! I had watched it every day for about a month. There was so much peace and joy that I found in watching that video. This dance ministry was different from others I had seen. They danced with such passion. They drew me in, and I felt a connection. I knew every dance move, and I even had my favorite dancers. Yet even with the peace the video gave me, I felt like I could not continue to live with the lifelong pain I carried every day.

Well, I did what I said I was going to do; I tried to take my life. I was found half dead by an out-of-town friend whom I had forgotten about. She would stay at my house when she came in town, and she had her own key. She happened to come in town the very day that I tried to take my life. I was rushed to the hospital and was there for about two weeks. When I finally regained consciousness, days after I arrived, I muttered the words "T. P. I. D". No one knew what that meant, and they thought I was still a little woozy. I knew exactly what I was saying. I mean, I had spent the last month with them every day. TPID, Total Praise In Dance! That's who I wanted to talk to. That's who

Kar'Michay Pope

I wanted to connect with. After leaving the hospital, I was placed in the behavioral center that I knew far too well. I was placed there, in the inpatient facility, for about a month.

When I was released from inpatient and returned home, I had received an email from the leader of TPID, and all she said was, "We care, and we are here for you." This was funny because she was the one dancer in the video that I didn't like! I felt like she was all about herself and that she cared more about her dance moves than God. I soon learned that this couldn't be further from the truth. Meanwhile, the dancer that I liked the most and thought I wanted to be like turned out to be much more normal than the pedestal I had put her on. So, over time, I became close to this lady, the leader of the dance ministry that I loved so much. The more we talked, she went from being the leader of the ministry, to my friend, to my sister, to "Sissy". We stayed in contact for years through emails and eventually phone calls. She called me sister and she was my Sissy. I even visited Huntsville and TPID two times. Sissy and the team would always encourage me to move there and start a new life. It sounded great, but I didn't know how to leave. I couldn't imagine life without my family, my uncle, and my pain.

Fast forward to 4 years after that first encounter with TPID and Sissy. I did it! I made the move, and I'm living with her and my new brother (her husband). A few short months after moving to Huntsville, we were on our way to church one Sunday, and out of the blue Sissy said, "Your brother and I need to have some sort of authority over you." I think she said this because, although I was living in their home, I was still just doing whatever I wanted. So I said, "Okay."

A little while later, another few months later, actually, I casually mentioned, "You guys are like my parents, why don't you adopt me?" I was just joking, but I think some part of me really meant it. My Sissy responded, "Your mother? I'm not old enough to be a mother!" She was serious about it, too. She said multiple times that she was just not old enough to have a grown daughter. She wasn't being mean about it; it was just the truth. She was right, as funny as she was saying it. She was not old enough to have a grown daughter. After all, in her words, she was only 23! LOL! She was in pure denial! Although we called each other sister, we for sure had a mother/daughter relationship. Neither of us knew what was in store for our relationship!

During all of this time, she and my brother fought physically, mentally, and spiritually against all the demons of my past that were inside of me. Every time we thought I was free, something else came up, and once again we... well, they... were fighting for me. Sissy would always tell me, "We're fighting for you, even if you won't fight for yourself." I must admit, I was tired. I was done. Years of pain, hurt, abuse, abandonment, mistreatment, hatred, and self-hate don't just go away when you move to another city. I hated myself for being free, yet still being in bondage. Nevertheless, they were on a mission for me to be free. They connected me with a good counselor, and for nine months they spent hours each day working with me: soothing me when I had flashbacks, making me speak positively to myself in the mirror, helping me end some of my self-sabotaging habits, teaching me that God really does love me, and so much more. On the last day of the ninth month, God spoke to them and said, "On this day you have labored and fought for nine months, and great is your reward." "You're seed," He said to my brother, "has entered into your womb," He said to my sister, "and you three have become a three-strand cord that shall never be broken." Trust me, that was a "wow" moment for all of us! After that, Sissy and Brother became Mom and Dad.

Not too long after that epic moment, my brother and Sissy had a deep conversation and came to the conclusion that I needed a real family. They recognized that I had never experienced love, and I needed to know what true love is. They talked it over, prayed to make the right decision, and I was called into the room. "We have something we want to tell you", they said, which to me meant it was something bad that they had to say. Instead, what came out of their mouths were some of the best words I could ever hear! "We are going to be your parents." I'm thinking, "Okay, you are already my parents." They replied, "No, we are going to adopt you, legally." I don't think I have ever cried that much with excitement!

They had already done some research to determine how to adopt an adult, so the lawyer was found pretty quickly. I went with my Sissy... oh wait! I mean... I went with my mom to talk to the lawyer, and he asked me how I felt about leaving my birth family and becoming theirs. I, of course, had no qualms about it! They were about to officially become my parents!! I get excited now just thinking about it! I have been given the best gift ever, and it wasn't even my birthday or Christmas. Fly me to the moon!! Here I am, a broken girl from a broken past, finally getting a loving family. They wanted me. They loved me. All this time, I thought I was unlovable and unwanted, but two people cared enough to save me, labor over me, and birth my new beginning.

Weeks later, we went before the judge, and he laughed and joked around with us as he was looking over the paperwork. My heart was racing even though I was smiling. I was so nervous that he would find something in there that would ruin the process, but he didn't! He looked at us, asked a few questions, and just like that… it was over! He looked at my parents and spoke those four words that changed my life forever, "You are her parents." He shook our hands and said, "Congratulations! You are a family." We left that courtroom with so much excitement! I mean, I knew in my head it was going to happen, I just didn't know for sure in my heart. My mom was jumping up and down with me, and my dad (OMG, I have a dad!) was even excited, which… if you knew my dad, you'd know that showing emotion doesn't come naturally for him. From that day forward, I was theirs and they were mine!

I even remember the day Dad first said, "I love you" when we hung up the phone. It was a sunny day, and I had just returned home from a counseling session. He called to make sure that all was well and I was safe. My mom said it all the time when we hung up the phone, but he had never said it. After he knew that I was okay, we ended the phone call, and he spoke those three words: "I love you." For most people, hearing those words is no big deal, but my daddy loved me! OMG, my daddy loved me! I called my mom as soon as we hung up to tell her, as if I was telling on him! LOL! "Mom," I said, "Dad just said I love you to me. He did realize it was me he was talking to, right? Or did he think I was you on the phone?" "Well, she said, "that's your dad. He does love you! Just because he doesn't express it like I do doesn't mean he doesn't love you." I was shaken! He loved me; he actually loved me! For a girl who never had love from a father and was used to men perverting love to me in a painful way, this was life-changing!

Not too long after that, we were on a family vacation (family vacation? Families actually take vacations??), and we were in the car. My parents had picked up the mail before we left, and Mom was going through it. She paused and nonchalantly said to me, "Here, you have some mail." It was pretty strange for me to have mail, so with curiosity, I opened up the envelope. There it was! My new birth certificate! I just stared at it! It had all of our names on it. It was official! Their names were listed as giving birth to me. We were a family before, but we were REALLY a family now, in all ways possible. Our lives together have been less than perfect or easy, and we have had to fight through so many things, but one thing has and will always remain true... we are a three-strand cord that shall never be broken!

Personal Discovery:

This is my story of redemption... my story of being saved from lifelong pain, abuse, disappointment, evil, and bondage to being shown unconditional love, protection, and an unbreakable family connection. My story is a miracle, but every story of redemption is miraculous.

1. What's your redemption situation or story?
2. What negative experiences from your past—big or small—have you been freed from, or are starting to let go of?
3. Oftentimes, you don't realize that someone is fighting for you, even when you don't feel like you can fight for yourself. Who has fought for you in your lifetime? Take a step back and see who's really in your corner. Allow yourself to receive the support they give you.
4. Looking back, I realize that God ordered my steps to TPID and to Huntsville, and I would have never come up with that on my own. Looking back over your life, in what ways do you realize now that God has ordered your steps?

Kar'Michay Pope

Story 2: A Pony Kind of Christmas

I never really had a Christmas growing up. Lyla, my mother, would always seem to run out of money right before the holiday, except for two specific years... those years were different, and not in a good way! When I was 5 years old, we received gifts from the angel tree before Christmas. I had gotten a music book and a $20 gift card to Walmart. You would have thought I hit the lottery as excited as I was! We also had gifts under the tree from Santa; we couldn't believe that Santa had not run out of money this year, as he had almost every year prior. After seeing my gifts under the tree for the few weeks leading up to Christmas, you can imagine how excited I was to be able to play with the music book and the gifts from Santa. I opened them and played with them all Christmas day. It was, by far, the best Christmas ever... until... for no apparent reason, right before bedtime, Lyla came into my room, grabbed my Christmas gifts, and told me to watch as she threw them in the fireplace. I didn't watch. I couldn't watch. I just sat in my room and cried. I was devastated. Why? Why were they gone, just like that? Here I am having the best Christmas ever, and it all of a sudden turned into the worst Christmas ever... even worse than the ones in which we didn't receive anything because Santa was out of money.

So now, at age 6, it's time for Christmas again. It's amazing how much a child tries to maintain hope even though they've been let down time after time! I had seen commercials about My Little Pony dolls throughout the year. I wanted those dolls so badly and had been asking Santa for them all Christmas season. And what did Lyla do? She got me some My Little Pony Dolls! She bought them before Christmas and showed them to me! Wow! The My Little Ponies that I wanted so bad were going to be mine Christmas day! You can't begin to imagine how excited this 6-year-old girl was for Christmas day. One pony was pink with a rainbow on its side, with blue hair. One was purple with rainbow colored hair. One was yellow with wings and pink hair, and the last one, which happened to be my favorite, was pink with red colored hair. Yes, you counted correctly… four ponies! Can you picture them? Can you feel my excitement? Then you can probably imagine how disappointed I was when Christmas morning came, and my My Little Pony dolls were nowhere to be found! Lyla had lifted my spirits just to crush them… again.

I hated Christmas from then on. No matter where I was or what home I was in, I didn't look forward to Christmas. I mean, how could I? Lyla did a great job of putting a hatred for the holiday in me. I mean, to be honest, I really don't remember Christmas most of my life after these two years. I hated it so much that I made a point not to put much energy into it and not to get myself excited about it. I knew how THAT would turn out! Throughout my childhood and adolescence, I was always scared that if I received a gift, it would soon be taken from me. Little did I know, however, that years later, there would be some redemption for my traumatic Christmas memories.

When I moved to Huntsville as an adult, I didn't realize I was moving into the home of someone who

Kar'Michay Pope

LOVES Christmas. Even today, I say that it looks like Santa Claus threw up in the house during the holiday season. (I'm sure that's because I still have a little distaste for Christmas after all those years of hating it.) It was my fourth Christmas with this new family, and boy, does this family have Christmas traditions! We each have a stocking hung that gets filled Christmas Eve night, we exchange a special ornament each year, my mom likes to drive around during the season looking at Christmas lights… I mean, it is like a real-life Hallmark movie without the baking of Christmas cookies… and then, a few years later, we started baking and decorating Christmas cookies! OMG, it just hit me! We are a Hallmark Christmas family!

On Christmas morning, we open stockings first. Each of our stockings has our names on them, and my stocking was red with a penguin on skis on it. There were so many neat little amazing things that I love in my stocking, and I was satisfied with Christmas after opening and going through it. I didn't have to have another gift! But, unlike growing up, I had multiple gifts under the tree to open, and being kind-of, not-really, but very-much-so OCD, it always took me the longest time to open my gifts. I mean, I can't just rip the paper!

I received so many of my favorite gifts like clothes, jewelry, tickets to Alabama gymnastics meets, and more. I opened gift after gift, wrapped in beautiful paper, and finally, it was time to open my last gift. I pried the bow loose, gently pulled the wrapping paper off, and OMG! I couldn't believe it! There, in front of me, were My Little Pony dolls, and this time I didn't just have four, I had six! I cried with excitement! After all those years, I FINALLY got my My Little Pony dolls back, and in that moment, I felt like a happy little girl, which was a feeling I didn't often have. I think my mom's eyes watered a little bit, too. My parents said, "We are replacing bad memories with good ones."

Christmas night, I kept looking at the ponies, scared to open them, out of fear that they were going to be taken. My mom came into my room and told me to open the ponies; I believe she even helped me open them. Right there and then, as old and adult as I was, I got down on the floor like an 8-year-old and played with my ponies to my heart's content... and they were never taken away. I went to bed and woke up the next morning, and the first thing I did was look for them. There they were! My My Little Pony dolls were still there, where I left them. To this day, I have them displayed in my room. Mom and Dad are serious about creating good memories to replace the bad ones, and this particular Christmas was no exception. I've had many great Christmases since I've been in Huntsville, but this one, a pony kind of Christmas, will stick with me for a lifetime!

Personal Discovery:

In this story, I suffered for so many years from the emotional trauma I experienced at Christmas. Yet, I had to learn that redemption is possible. When things seem bleak and it seems that everything is working against you, something unexpected can happen that can be greater than you thought possible.

1. What does redemption mean to you personally?

2. Do you feel like you are worthy of experiencing redemption in areas of your life that have experienced trauma? Why or why not?

3. Is there something that you've given up on that you should consider hoping for again?

4. I had a hard time believing that my new parents wouldn't treat me like Lyla did. Is there something God is revealing to you that you have a hard time trusting or believing in?

Story 3: The Mystery Man

I was called into a room. It was dark. The light was broken. I had been awakened out of my sleep and told to go wash my face. After that, I was to meet him in the room. I had so many different emotions going on inside of me. I had heard he was coming over, but he took so long that I fell asleep. I really thought he was not actually coming. So here I am now, a 7-year-old, making my half-sleep self go wash my face so that I can go into this dark room as directed. I entered the room and then… I just stood there, confused about why we were in the dark. All of a sudden, my thoughts shifted to, "Will this mystery man like me? "Will he want me in his life?" "Will he be sorry for leaving me?"

Then it happens. He walks into the room. Of course, it's dark, so all I can see is a shadow of a tall, thin man. For a moment, I was super scared. In that moment, I forgot that I was meeting my "dad", and I feared that it was just another man there to hurt me. Truth is, I had no faith that he wasn't there to hurt me… that he wasn't just like all the other men that just wanted to hurt me. This mystery man—what was he going to say to me? How was he going to act with me? And what was I going to say to him? The anticipation, the fear, the questions! I felt it all at the same time. Then, the first thing he does when he walks into the room is say, "Hi, I'm your dad."

As we're still in the dark, and I've now heard his voice for the first time, he hugs me, and though I hugged him back, I felt no warmth… no true love. I was hugging a complete stranger, and it definitely felt like it. All the warm fuzzy feelings that I thought I would feel were not there, and there were no feelings of "finally I am complete!" "You have a brother and sister that I want you to meet," he said. "I'm going to come pick you up to see them and go swimming, you know, so you can all get to know each other," he continued. All this sounded sweet to the ear, but in my heart, there was only sadness. Sadness, because I wanted so badly to believe his words. I wanted so bad to finally be accepted by someone, anyone, but especially my "dad". However, all I felt inside was the long list of things he didn't say... things like "I love you," "I'm sorry," "I am here now," or "I'm going to take care of you now." These words seemed to be stuck somewhere other than in his heart and able to come out of his mouth.

Once again, I was rejected, and he never had to tell me I was because I felt it. It felt all too familiar and all too real. This mystery man left as quickly as he came. I was right to think he was going to hurt me like so many of the men had before him. He took something that the others couldn't. He took my hope: my hope in feeling as if this time I was going to be chosen for a reason other than the use of my body; my hope that this time I was going to be loved by a parent without having to pay something in return. Yeah, like most of the men I had ever come in contact with, he took way more than he gave me. This experience taught me that they, everyone, was right when they made me believe that I wasn't worth it.

I didn't hear from the mystery man for many years. Every time I thought things were going to change and he would become at least a little bit of a "dad", he proved me wrong. I eventually came to the conclusion that he always showed me who he was; I just didn't believe or want to believe him. My vision of a father was tarnished by a stranger in the night, whose face I never saw, all those years ago, and it left me with feelings of never being good enough and never being wanted. This mystery man remained a mystery throughout most of my life, and, at the time of this writing, I've still never seen his face in person. In this case, I'm content with leaving the mystery unsolved.

Personal Discovery:

In this story, there was a lot of anticipation of possible events. I was both excited and nervous. Would it be the outcome that I am wanting, or would it be yet another disappointment? Anticipation is a strange space to live in, caught between what is and what could be. Sometimes it felt like hope, like the promise of something better just ahead. Other times, it felt like anxiety, my mind racing with "what ifs," bracing for disappointment, afraid to want too much. I didn't realize, until I began my healing journey, how much emotional energy I spent waiting... for answers, for healing, for peace, for permission to feel joy without fearing it would be taken away. But I've learned that anticipation isn't just about what's coming, it's also a mirror, showing me what I long for, what I fear, and where I still need trust. It's taught me patience, resilience, and the importance of staying present even when my heart is leaning forward into the future. Now, I'm learning to hold anticipation more gently—not as pressure or fear, but as a quiet readiness. I may not know what's next, but I know who I am as I wait, and that is its own kind of strength.

1. How do you typically feel, both physically and emotionally, when you're waiting for something important to happen?
2. What emotions come up when you think about the future? Why do you think those emotions are the ones that arise?
3. What kind of thoughts do you have when you're anticipating an outcome? What steps can you take to maintain control of your thoughts during these times?
4. How do your expectations influence your actual experience when the anticipated event occurs?

Story 4: Angel of My Dreams

The day started just like every other day... yelling through the house to wake us up, eating cereal, and getting hit for eating too slowly. Then off to school. I was in first grade, and my teacher's name was Ms. Brown. I loved her so much! She always saved me an extra snack to take home.

I was alone. I was always alone. I always felt alone, too. I came home early this day because I didn't feel well. Lyla was upset, of course. She was always upset with me. I was told to go to bed while her friend came over. I was so scared because every time she said a friend was coming over, my treasure box hurt. This time was a little different. Her friend came into my room and walked right out. I never thought this would happen! I fell asleep and had the scariest yet best dream ever!

In my dream, I was surrounded by fire, and there were lots of scary voices yelling at me to come with them. They were screaming at me very, very loudly. Then, out of nowhere, there was a lady reaching out to me. She was not on fire; instead, she was surrounded by light. With her hands outstretched, she was telling me to come to her, but that's all I could see... her face and her hands. I didn't want to trust her, but she seemed so good and peaceful. After a bit of hesitation, I went to her. As I walked towards her, the loud, screaming voices quieted, and she became brighter. The closer I got to her, the lighter it became, until I could only see light and couldn't really see her face. Being in the light with her was peaceful, and I felt so safe there! When I woke up, I started calling this beautiful lady "Angel".

I had this exact same dream twice, on this day and about a year or two later. Of all the dreams I've had growing up, this one always stuck with me, and I can remember it vividly. I remember Angel's face, her voice, and the light and peace that surrounded her. Many years later, after I was rescued from my crazy family, moved to Huntsville, connected with Sissy and her Husband ("Brother"), who later became my mom and dad, I had this dream a third time... except it was not a dream!

I woke up in the middle of the night, one night, in my bedroom in Huntsville, to a face that I knew all too well. I couldn't believe my eyes! I couldn't believe that Angel was standing above me. I mean, was this just a figment of my imagination; was I having the dream again? I didn't see the fire this time, only Angel. Was this really the Angel of my dreams? The room was pitch black, and her face seemed to glow. That's what made me realize. Oh goodness, this is truly the Angel! All of these months and years, I've seen her face and didn't realize that THAT was the same face I had seen in the dreams 14 years prior as a six-year-old, hurting, abused girl. It was Sissy! When I woke up and saw her, I asked her one simple question, "What's your name?" She, having no idea about my dream from years ago, answered, "My name is Angel, what's yours?"

Personal Discovery:

In this story I received, what I did not know then, was a vision of what was to come. When I first received the vision, it felt too big, too distant, too unrealistic that it could happen for me. Like a dream that was meant for someone stronger, holier, more ready than me. I carried it quietly, almost afraid to hope. But even when I doubted, God didn't. And when it finally came to pass, I realized it was never about how worthy I felt. It was about how faithful He is. What I thought was impossible was already written. I just had to grow into it.

1. What was the moment you realized a vision you were given was coming true?
2. What did this experience teach you about trust and timing?
3. How did it shape your faith, identity, or purpose going forward?
4. What advice would you give to someone who feels like they've received a vision but are waiting for it to be fulfilled?

Kar'Michay Pope

Story 5: Back to the Basics?

(Content Warning: This story contains descriptions of sexual abuse and/or violence. Please take care of yourself while reading.)

It has been discovered that every child is entitled and needs to have their basic needs met. The basic levels of needs, according to Abraham Maslow's hierarchy, include physiological needs, safety needs, belongingness and love needs, and esteem needs. However, for me as a young girl, there was no entitlement when it came to basic needs. I grew up believing everyone was like me, everyone felt like I felt, everyone was without like I was. This, I found out later, was far from the case. Yes, while others may have gone through pain of some type, their basic needs were generally met in at least one or two areas, while mine were not. It was especially like this for me at age eight, although I experienced it many other years. This is the year Fred came into the picture.

Fred was genuinely nice to me and my siblings and would buy us things that we wanted. He even bought us things we didn't ask for, until one day when everything changed… I made him mad. Well, it was not I who made him mad; it was my brother, but of course, I was not going to let my brother get in trouble. So, I said it was I who flooded the bathtub. He whipped me with a belt buckle, and it caught my finger and broke it. When I yelled in agony, the whipping didn't stop; I just kept getting hit with the buckle side of the belt. I cried out for Lyla to help me, but, as usual, she was getting high and never even knew what was going on. After he finished beating me, he said,

"Now you will listen or else you will get the same whooping the next time." "Yes, Sir," I whimpered through the tears and pain. He gave me a bag of frozen peas to put on my hand and said, "Ain't nothing wrong with you, so shut up!"

I secretly called Granny. She came and got me to take me to the hospital, and it was determined that I indeed had a broken hand. "What?!" I thought, "I went to the doctor, and someone believed me?!" This was at least one of my basic needs that was met that day, although it is not in Maslow's hierarchy: I called someone, they came to see about me, and my story was believed. For a brief moment, I felt that there was a glimmer of safety and hope in my life. However, that glimmer was indeed faint and didn't last long.

When I returned home, I had to get undressed and be sexually molested by Fred as a punishment for calling my granny. This kind of behavior lasted for about four days. I was not able to leave the house, be near the phone, or talk to Lyla. I learned my lesson in those four days and in the days and weeks to come. No one in the house went to work, because they didn't need to. They got a check and food stamps every month. I was never safe, nor did I ever have control over my own body. Everyone seemed to have authority and control to do whatever they wanted to do to me, and I didn't. So, the second basic need of security and safety... that every child needs... nope! This eight-year-old didn't have it.

We moved out of the house that year because, as I was told, they didn't want us there as I got older. I realize now, we got kicked out. So, the five of us, Lyla, my three siblings, and I, lived in the car through winter. We were told that we needed to be grateful to have a "fun" place to live. I was eight, my brothers were six and five, and my sister was two. All of us would get left in the car by Lyla so often. We would play games, cry, and wander outside of the car… anything to pass that time. Of course, it was my responsibility to make sure everyone was okay, but I wasn't okay. I wasn't okay then, and I wasn't okay for many, many years to come. I was told so many times that it was my fault that we had to leave that house. I was told how much I wasn't loved or worthy to be cared for. During this time, the first and most basic need, the physiological needs of food, water, warmth, and rest, were few and far between for us.

Age eight was also the year that truly made me aware that my body was used as payment to men so that we could eat, and sometimes Lyla spent most of the money I made on drugs… most of the time. Fred was still in the picture, and we eventually moved into a motel. That motel had roaches EVERYWHERE. We stayed there for a few months, and it felt like forever. Men would come and go, and I was forced to be with them, and then I'd see them give money to Lyla. I mean, did they know I was eight? Come on now! I may have looked 11, but even still, I was a child… a broken and used child! Meanwhile, when Fred came, I was forced to have sex with him with no payment to follow that I knew of.

I got slapped and punched in the face more times that year than any other year that I can remember. I was always bruised up. One time, I saw Lyla get dragged out of the motel by her hair by Fred, and when I tried to stop it, I was backhanded. Folks began to gather in the parking lot to watch her being beaten, and no one would help her. No one even tried; they just stood there, oohing and ahing and watching. She was beaten up in the parking lot, and no one cared. Of course, I was forced to sleep with him when he finished beating her up because I tried to help her. It never went well when I tried to help Lyla.

Lyla left the motel that day, and I was forced to remain there to take care of my siblings alone. I had to sleep with Fred every day to make sure we had a place to stay. She was gone for three months. I was scared and alone. The third basic need, the need for belongingness and love, was absent from me and my life. The responsibility of these three other humans in my care, whom I loved, was terrifying. I didn't want anything to happen to them, and it would be my fault if it did. We ate lots of ramen noodles. I mean, lots of them! I would go to the corner store and steal them at first, but after a while, the guy at the corner store would just give the ramen noodles and bread to me. He would say, "You don't have to steal, you can just ask me for it." I'm sure, as an eight-year-old, I wasn't very inconspicuous in how I would steal food. I just needed to make sure my sibling could eat. Fred would sometimes bring stuff like pull-ups for my baby sister or food for us when he came. Every time he brought something, he would say, "Now you know what that means." It seemed that nothing was free, but he was going to force his body on me whether he was bringing something to me or not. I, as an eight-year-old, made sure that my three younger siblings were fed, had a place to stay, and were generally taken care of. You would think that I would be thanked, patted on the back, applauded, or in some way made to feel like I was doing something well. No! The fourth basic need, the need for esteem, the need to feel accomplishment, achievement, or good performance, was non-existent. I never felt like I did the right thing, and I never had the wherewithal to give myself credit for the adult-like responsibility I was taking on and mastering.

Looking back, I realize that the majority of the people staying at the motel were drug addicts and prostitutes. It was an atmosphere that made me scared to go anywhere, and I always took my siblings with me when I went places. It was just too unsafe to leave them at the motel... both for them and for me. I thought Lyla would never come back. This was not the first time that Lyla left us and was gone for however long she wanted to go, and it wouldn't be the last. The daily rapes by Fred didn't stop until after Lyla returned, we moved from the motel to one of Lyla's friends' houses, and we were then taken and placed in foster care. I don't know how long that ended up being... maybe 5 months?

I hated being eight, and I thought I would never be free. It went from beatings and a broken finger to five of us living in a car to raising my siblings in that horrible motel. To be honest, I'd rather be back in the cramped car than be stuck in a single room getting raped every day. My family didn't love me, and I had no friends or support. Everyone always says that it is good to go back to the basics, but what basis do I have to go back to? What does that mean for me?

Personal Discovery:

According to Maslow, the basic needs are:

- Physiological – food, water, shelter, etc.
- Safety/Security – health, wellness, protection from injury/harm, etc.
- Love/Belonging – love, acceptance, family connection, friendships, etc.
- Esteem – appreciation, respect, accomplishment, etc.

I realize that many of my basic needs, especially for safety, comfort, and emotional connection, were not consistently met. Growing up, I often had to minimize what I needed to feel loved or accepted. As a result, I learned to suppress my needs and take care of others instead. This has left me feeling disconnected from myself, uncertain about what I truly need, and sometimes ashamed for even having needs at all. Now, I'm slowly learning to acknowledge those unmet needs with compassion, and I'm starting to believe that I deserve to have them met, not just by others, but by myself too.

1. What would it look like to fully honor all of your needs today?
2. If you could give your younger self what they needed most, what would that be, and how would you provide it?
3. In what situations do you find it hard to even recognize your needs?
4. How do you cope when your needs aren't met, and what steps can you take to begin to meet your basic needs right now?

Story 6: A Southern Grandmother

Every other year, we spent Christmas in Houston with my mom's mom. This year was my first time going. I was super nervous to meet her as a true granddaughter after the adoption. I had met her once before, but this was the first time I would be spending any real time with her. This was my first time flying to Houston, so I really didn't know what to expect. Though it was winter, it was also the South, so I packed shorts and pants. I honestly did not want to go because I didn't know if she was going to like me or even accept me. I had no idea what was gonna happen when I got there. However, with a bit of worry and unsurety, I packed my suitcase and made my way, along with my family, to the airport. We landed in Houston and had to make a stop at the hotel. When we got to the hotel, we unpacked and settled into our new home away from home for the week. Then it was time to meet her. My nerves were bad! I was shaking, and my heart was racing. I had to talk myself into breathing. I kept asking my mom how she is going to be. All she kept telling me was to calm down and that it was going to be all good. She even prayed with me to calm me down.

We pulled into the driveway, me not wanting to get out of the car… I started panicking. I finally got out of the car with much hesitation. I just wanted to run away. However, when she opened the door, all fear and anxiousness went away immediately. The warm big hugs and big smile… everything was amazing. It was as if God knew what to do for me to be OK. She squeezed me as if I had known her for years, she hugged me with the kind of hug I had never felt before - the kind of hug that I needed to receive my entire life. She kissed me on the cheek and welcomed me into her home as if I were royalty. Was this going to be my experience for the next week? We spent so much time together. It was full of her just wanting to get to know me, and me wanting to get to know her. I cannot believe that this was the one that I was so afraid to meet!

We laughed and talked the entire time. All I wanted to do was sit under her and absorb all her love and wisdom. It was amazing! I no longer cared why we were there. I loved this woman, and I could tell that she loved me too. I wanted to stay forever the moment she told me that she was my Nana and that I was her grandbaby forever. You would have thought she just gave me a million dollars, as happy as I was. I felt every word and truly believed it in my heart. When we got to the end of the week and it was time to go, we gave our hugs and kisses and got in the car. Suddenly, it hit me. We were leaving, we were leaving, and I didn't want to go. The little girl inside of me wanted answers. Why were we leaving, and why did we have to go? Can she come with us? Can I stay with her? I cried all the way back to the hotel. I was devastated. I didn't want to leave what I just got. I did not want to leave the comfort and the love that I experienced. Honestly, I had never, ever experienced a love and acceptance like that before, and my heart yearned for it. I cried and cried. I mean, I toddler-cried! My mom comforted me and let me know that I would see her again and that she was not going anywhere. At first, I argued with her. It was almost like I went from the comforting feeling of love and acceptance to that oh so familiar feeling of being abandoned again, and that was not a good exchange of feelings! We flew out the next morning, and it wasn't until we were on the plane that I found peace in my heart, knowing that this warm, accepting, beautiful soul was forever my Nana, my southern grandmother, and I was forever her grandbaby.

Personal Discovery:

In this story, I realized that I spent so long bracing myself for the moment they'd turn away, when they'd see too much, or not enough, and decide that I didn't belong. But they didn't. They stayed; she stayed. And, in that quiet, steady acceptance, I realized that fear wasn't proof that I didn't deserve love; it was just a scar from the times I didn't receive it. Being accepted didn't erase the fear, but it began to rewrite the story.

1. What fears come up when you think about not being accepted?
2. Do you believe you have to earn acceptance?
3. Where do you believe your need for acceptance comes from?
4. What would it mean if someone didn't accept you? Does that change your worth?

Story 7: The Spiritual One

Frilly socks with the matching outfit and shoes —
this is how she presented herself every day. I mean, there
was not a day that she was not put together from head to
toe. Click clack — the sound of her heels hitting the ground
as she pranced down the hallway. Okay, maybe it was not
a prance; she just walked with purpose. There was no
wondering if she took her job seriously, because it showed
in everything that she did. Not only did she walk with
purpose, but she also carried herself with confidence — a
confidence I had only seen in my mom until then. She did
not act as if she were above or better than anyone. I could
just tell that there was something different about her. She
was different in a weird, not-so-weird way. One could tell
that she was not just an average person. I was in my first
"real" job as a social worker after receiving my master's in
social work. There were several of us who started working
at this job and went through orientation together. I was
excited and nervous at the same time, and I checked
everyone out carefully to make sure I understood my
surroundings.

Then one day it hit me! I found out that she goes to
church with someone I know. "That's it, that's it!" I said to
myself. She is a Christian! She is spiritual. That's why she
appears so different. Funny thing is, we never talked about
God, or church, or anything that would make me believe
that she was more than just a church attender. I just knew
that she was more than that. Something about her spirit

jumped right at me and told me all that I needed to know; therefore, she became known to me as The Spiritual One.

Though she was super nice and sweet, there was something about her I did not like. I wanted no part of being her friend, let alone allowing her to get close to me. This was the same thing I thought about my mom before she was my mom. Funny how the devil jumps in when God has something for you, and makes you think you're doing the right thing. I avoided her at all costs. I mean, I spoke when I saw her, but just chit-chatting was not going to happen. Boy, was I in for a surprise! God was working things, and I had no idea that He was even in the midst. She checked on me quite often to see how I was doing, and I always tried to give the "I'm fine" answer. Until one day, I was going through it, and I had no one to talk to. I did not trust people, and therefore, I did not want to just share my personal life with coworkers. Out of desperation and needing to talk to someone, I wrote her a note on a card and gave it to her. Now I don't remember what that note said, but what I do know is that it had to be God who encouraged me to give it to her. We started talking after that and made a deeper connection than I ever thought I wanted to make.

Then, one day, we had a staff meeting at work. Our boss messed up the food order, so we ended up eating wings from a nearby wing restaurant instead of pizza. We loved those wings so much that we got them almost every day for lunch. We would take turns going out for wings, and we'd let each other know where we were going and bring the other food. This went on for a little while, and we became closer and closer. Although I had been in

Huntsville for over ten years by this time, I still found myself struggling… fighting sometimes to want to live. I know that sounds crazy to those on the outside. "If you've moved and you're safe, what's the problem?" I can hear y'all saying it now! To be honest, making a change on the outside is great and important. The change that must be made on the inside… whew! That takes so much longer and is so very hard. I had been in counseling for years at this point, and I still had internal struggles of feeling worthless, hopeless, empty, not enough, unseen, and so much more. So, after The Spiritual One was there for me when I wrote her the note, she was also there during another moment where I was struggling with life. She walked with me and talked me through that moment as well, which made us grow even closer. I did not know what I needed for myself, my well-being, my mental health at that time, and apparently, I needed The Spiritual One in my life.

Then one day she told me that she was leaving the job, and I was shocked and upset. "Now wait a minute," I said to myself. "How did this happen? How did I go from never wanting to have anything to do with The Spiritual One to feeling like my sister was leaving me?" I still did not know that God was up to something. As time went on, we grew closer. I realized that she is truly the spiritual one, always ready to shout praises to the Lord at any given moment. Yet I've come to appreciate that she is so much more than that. She is my sister, and I wouldn't have it any other way. I am a better me because of her. I'm blessed to have three amazing "sisters" who have come into my life

Kar'Michay Pope

since moving to Huntsville… just another testament to the miraculous work God has done for me!

When I was in yet another moment of severe depression and felt as if there was nothing left to live for, she was there to walk me through. From walking three miles with me while I poured out my pain to listening intently to me when I was driving around lost, describing my pain, my sister has been there. I cannot remember a time when she said to me, "You're too much to deal with" or "I can't be there for you." Not once has she turned her back on me. Since the day I met her with her frilly socks at work, she has sat with me, lay next to me, held me as I cried, prayed for me, and fought me for me. For all of these things and for the beautiful way she loves me, I am eternally grateful.

Personal Discovery:

In this story, I did not know that God was working on my behalf to place a lifelong sister-friend in my life. Once again, He was fighting against me to help me. Some people come into your life like a whisper, not loud, not planned, not wrapped in fireworks. At first, I didn't even realize how much I needed her. I wasn't looking for a friend, let alone a sister. I was too focused on surviving, healing, and holding myself together. But somehow, she showed up, gently, patiently, without trying to fix me, just offering space to be seen. I didn't know it then, but her presence was a turning point in my life. It wasn't in grand gestures; it was in being understood without having to explain everything… in laughter that I hadn't felt so deeply in years… in safety that didn't demand anything from me. Over time, I realized: this person was a gift I didn't ask for, but one my heart had been quietly longing for all along. She reminded me that not all healing happens in solitude. Sometimes, it arrives in the form of someone who sees the parts of you that you've hidden, even from yourself, and stays. And now, when I look back, I don't question the timing. I just feel grateful that God gave me exactly what I needed before I even knew how to ask for it.

1. What is something or someone that you know is good for you that you often avoid?

2. Is there a part of you that feels like you don't deserve good things? What are the steps you can take to love and heal that part of you?

3. Does avoidance of good and hope for yourself connect to an experience where "good" didn't feel safe or reliable? If so, describe that situation and share it with a trusted friend or counselor.

4. What steps can you take to forgive yourself for the times you've avoided or delayed your growth or care?

Story 8: A Mystery No More

When he called, I never knew what he was going to say. Though we had been talking off and on for a few years now, I was never really sold on the fact that he was my father and actually wanted a relationship with me. The same thoughts I had when I met him in a dark room at the age of 7, I was having now. "Was he just gonna turn out to be like the rest of the men in my life?" I had finally been given a daddy, so having this man in my life who was biologically my father made me question if I had to choose between the two, cause if it came down to it, my daddy would have won, hands down. My daddy, though he had not been my daddy long, was the one to fight for me, with me, and fight what came against me spiritually. Ever since he adopted me, he redefined what fatherhood means for me... in a good way. So, I didn't want to have to choose. Mystery man was new, and though conversations were generally always positive, I was still afraid that he too would one day hurt me.

This day he called with some exciting news. He was getting married to the love of his life, in his words, and he was telling me all about it. He told me how his fiancée was going to call me because she wanted me to be involved in the wedding in some way. I was at a loss for words. This lady, whom I had never even spoken to, wanted me to be a part of a day that would be etched in history forever. It was a big deal to me. We talked, and I fell in love with her spirit! She was so gentle, so welcoming, so warm, and so full of hope that we would have a relationship. She asked me to be her bridesmaid, and I thought about it, and with a little hesitation, I said yes.

I was so excited to be asked that I did not think about what it all meant. Not only was I going to be meeting her for the first time, but I was essentially seeing him face-to-face for the very first time. My stomach was in knots leading up to this big event. I had to fly to California for the wedding. When I got there, I was second-guessing myself in all kinds of ways. Was this the right thing to be doing? What if she didn't like me for real? What if he didn't really want me there? I was literally having a panic attack walking into the karaoke bar where we were all supposed to meet. They were so gracious to invite my parents to the wedding so that I did not feel overwhelmed, and I'm so glad they did. However, feeling overwhelmed was an understatement.

I had, for years, been working on forgiveness from my past, and, of course, he was included in that work. I had been so angry at him for getting Lyla pregnant in the first place at such a young age, but then to add insult to injury, he denied me. When I had talked to him throughout the years on the phone, I learned that he was willing to raise a son whom he did not know for sure was his. So, what about me was so wrong that he didn't want me? I had prayed for answers; I had prayed for closure. On my healing journey, I realized that it was not about me; it was about him and the work that he had to do within himself. His not wanting me was not a reflection of me; it was a reflection of who he was at that time. So here I was, now a more healed adult (though that didn't stop the panic attacks), about to meet the man who had been a physical mystery the majority of my life. I had done the work to heal; question was... had he?

I walked in with my parents, and I just waited until I saw them. I knew what he looked like from pictures at my Nanu's house. I was getting sick to my stomach with the anxiety that I was feeling. My mom could see how nervous I was and hugged me and told me that it was all going to be okay. Finally, I saw him walking into the place, and I knew it was him. As he and his fiancée began to walk inside and towards the area where they were going to sit, I stood and walked toward him. I don't know what made me do that! I was so nervous, there were no thoughtful movements – just impulsive actions. The look on his face surprised me and gave me so much peace. He had the "finally we are together" look. Now, I don't know what he was really thinking, but to me it was an amazing feeling. So much relief in comparison to the anxiety and panic I had been feeling. Tears began to flow, and it seemed like all those warm feelings that I thought and hoped I would feel when I hugged him in that dark room as a child were there. Finally, it was real, and he wanted me as much as I didn't know I wanted him in my life. He hugged me. He hugged me for a very long time, and the tears continued to flow. I then saw and hugged his fiancée, who would later affectionately be called Momma Sylvia, and she was just as pure and genuine as she was on the phone.

The next day was the wedding, and it was simply beautiful, and the fact that I was there because I was wanted and thought about made me feel so very loved. The mystery man was a mystery no more, and for the first time, I did not feel like I had to choose between my father and my daddy. I could have them both. I could love them equally yet differently. I was their daughter, and that's all that mattered. I was loved and wanted by two safe men, who didn't choose me for what I could do for them, and didn't choose me for my body. They chose me from a place of pure, fatherly, Godly love. The more I talk to my father, the more I'm getting to know him. He even gave me a safe space to open up and tell him how I was feeling growing up without him and the anger I had carried inside for so many years. He listened and understood, which gave me more peace. I realized that we are much more alike than we are different. However, he may come in second to Momma Sylvia. Overall, this was a mystery worth being solved.

Personal Discovery:

In this story, I did not see it coming. The moment something good slipped quietly into my life when I least expected it. After everything I went through surrounding this father situation, I had learned to brace for disappointment. But that not-so-small, unexpected joy reminded me: life is not made of just what breaks us. Sometimes, without warning, it offers something beautiful too.

1. Can you recall a time when something unexpectedly good happened?
2. How did this surprise shift your mood or perspective?

3. How did you feel when you first realized it was a blessing?
4. What are your current struggles that might carry hidden blessings?

The

Caterpillar

2 Peter 3:18 "But grow in the grace and knowledge of our Lord and Savior Jesus Christ. To him be glory both now and forever! Amen."

Growth / Struggle / Learning
(Getting through what should have killed me)

In this stage, there's nothing to shield the caterpillar from the world, no armor, no wings, just vulnerability. It crawls through life exposed, focused solely on survival, gathering what it needs to one day become something more. This section represents the times in my life when things were at their lowest, when I felt unprotected, unseen, or overwhelmed. These are the seasons of hardship, heartbreak, and hustle, when I was simply trying to make it through. But even in survival, there is purpose. These stories reflect not only the struggle, but also the quiet strength it took to keep going and the hope that a better stage was still ahead.

Story 9: Is God Real?

(Content Warning: This story contains descriptions of sexual abuse and/or violence. Please take care of yourself while reading.)

I used to wonder if God was really real. Was He the kind of compassionate God everyone always talked about? To me, God was just a man who sat in heaven, looking down with a magnifying glass that burned people like bullies burn ants. I just couldn't imagine an all-knowing, all-caring, all-seeing, all-loving God that would sit there and watch His child get hurt time after time after time. And what do I mean by "get hurt"? Well, I've since learned that it was way more than most people can even imagine. Let me tell you!

I remember his house almost as if I remember my own, except he had no flower wallpaper on the wall. I was 5 years old. The house reeked with the smell of pee. The walls were cream, and there were a couple of pictures of a strange man with long hair on them. I found out later who that strange man was: Bob Marley. I remember the house being smoky, and it was hard to breathe, even if I didn't have asthma.

In the bedroom, there were jars with straws in them, which I later found out were used for crack cocaine. This room stunk even beyond the pee odor! It smelled like someone had boo-booed on himself or in a corner of the room. The walls were brown with cream stripes. The man whose picture was on the walls in the living room was not in this room. There was no bed; only four chairs. The room was dirty with trash and beer bottles on the floor.

Kar'Michay Pope

My asthma in this smoky house had me coughing a whole lot. Mommy came in the room with big eyes and said, "Baby, just stay in here; I'll be right back. My friend is going to come watch you. I'll be in the next room." The only thing I could do was sit on the floor until I fell asleep. What I woke up to was a strange man pulling down my pants, rubbing my treasure box and kissing me. His lips felt like sharp rocks; his tongue tasted like a drink that I had snuck that was Mommy's. Anyways, it was nasty! He told me to touch his treasure box, which felt slimy like a worm. Gross! I didn't want to touch it, but he said I was going to get hit if I didn't. The next thing I knew, he put his treasure box on my face and pee-peed on it, except it didn't smell like peepee. It was all over me: on my hair, on my face, on my chest, everywhere. He said, "You're being a good girl now. Just breathe now. Do as I say. You're going to like it, I promise." He pulled me closer to him and put his treasure box in my treasure box. I started screaming, and he grabbed me by the throat, slapped me, and told me to shut up. I couldn't breathe, and I was in so much pain. The next thing I remember was waking up, and blood was all over my pants.

I cried out for Mommy, but she never came. I kept yelling for her. She never came. The next thing I remember... it was dark outside, and I was riding in a big car that made noise. A man who was sitting next to me was saying, "Sweetheart, you're going to be OK now." I told him it hurt really bad. My treasure box really hurt bad! When I woke up, because I think I fell asleep, there were wires everywhere on me. My treasure box didn't hurt so very bad anymore, just a little. Auntie Tiffany, who was really not an auntie but a friend of Mommy, was there and told me to tell everyone that I was with her. "Tell them you were playing on the bars and fell and hurt your treasure box," she said. I said, "Yes, ma'am." I guess this is where lying about what happens to me began.

I stayed in that place for a long time. They asked me what happened. I told them what Auntie told me to say, "I was playing in the bars and it hurt my treasure box." Then this lady wearing a white shirt came in and said, "You can tell me the truth, did someone hurt you down there?" She reached as if to touch me there. I screamed, "Please, PLEASE don't hurt my treasure box again!" "She said, "So who touched your treasure box? I, in tears, said, "Nobody. I fell and hurt my treasure box." I told this to everyone who asked me. I saw the lady talking to Auntie Tiffany. I didn't know what she said, but Auntie looked very sad. The lady in the white shirt told me that it was okay to go to sleep, and that's what I did.

So, tell me why I should have believed in God, why I should have trusted him? Why should I have thought He was loving and caring? Why would I not ask, "Is God real?" I mean, I didn't know. I didn't feel Him with me, and I certainly didn't feel like He was saving me.

Personal Discovery:

Please take a moment to gather yourself, as I know my story and my trauma can be overwhelming. I'm thankful that I made it through such unfathomable trauma. In this story, I questioned if God was real, and I couldn't understand how a real and good God could allow all that happened to me. After the many years of abuse I experienced, this story being one of the first, I carried a question heavier than the pain itself: if God is real, where was He? In the moments I felt most broken, most forgotten, I searched for signs, something, anything, to prove I wasn't completely alone. I wrestled with silence, with prayers that felt unanswered, with the ache of believing in something I couldn't feel. For a long time, I thought God's absence meant I wasn't worth saving. But somewhere in the quiet, in the slow work of healing, I began to feel something different—not a voice from the sky, but a whisper from within. Every time I chose to keep going, to speak the truth, to love myself a little more, I saw God in that... not in the way I expected, but in the strength I didn't know I had. I may never have all the answers, but now I know this: my trauma and survival were never proof of God's absence; they were proof of my resilience, and maybe, just maybe, of someone greater walking with me all along.

1. In what ways has your pain affected your sense of hope, trust, or faith?
2. Name a time that you thought God had ignored or forgotten you, but you can look back and realize that He was actually with you through the situation.
3. What strengths do you have that will help you through very painful situations?
4. What does it look like to trust God even when your past seems unforgettable and your future seems uncertain?

Story 10: Shattered Trust

(Content Warning: This story contains descriptions of sexual abuse and/or violence. Please take care of yourself while reading.)

I believe I was three when the abuse started, if not before. They say that traumatic events are memories that linger in your brain. They leave an imprint in the crevices of the brain. Well, at the age of seven, I gained an imprint of one of the more intense abusive moments of my childhood.

I remember it as if it had just happened yesterday. The wallpaper was beige with pink flowers and green leaves. The smell of strawberry incense, to cover the smell of marijuana, permeated the whole house. Loud music was playing from the back room that never seemed to drown out the episode of *Star Trek* that was playing in the living room. "TT, come here!" was what I heard. I got up as quickly as I could and ran to see why my name was being called. A slap across the face... that's what I was met with. "Don't run in my &#@!! House! You know better!!" she said with so much anger. "I'm sorry, mommy. I'm really sorry," I said.

She then told me that if I wanted to make up for running in the house, I needed to go in the room with her friend and do whatever he wanted me to do. I said, "Yes, ma'am!" I wanted so badly to make her not mad at me anymore that whatever she wanted me to do, I was willing to do. So, into the room I went. The walls were repainted in this bluish color. It was missing paint where my bed was. This was because my bed scratched the wall. The TV was on *Tom and Jerry*. I thought this was going to be fun, "We're just going to sit here on the bed and watch TV." No. This was not the case at all!

"Take off your clothes, sweetheart," the strange man said. Mommy told me to do whatever he wanted, so with much fear, I obliged. "Lie on the bed now and watch your show, OK?" "Yes, sir," I replied. I thought it was strange to be watching TV with no clothes on, but Mommy said to do whatever he wanted, so, "Okay," I thought. The next thing I remember was the most excruciating pain I had ever felt. I screamed in pain! His hand covered my mouth, and he told me to shut up — it will be over soon. To me, it was not soon at all. It felt like a whole lifetime went by. It hurt so bad! Why was it hurting so very badly? He got up, wiped himself off, gave me the bloodstained towel, and told me to clean myself. Blood was pouring out of me like a faucet that I couldn't turn off.

I got in the tub Mommy had filled with water for me, and OH, how that burned! My fragile seven-year-old body was left broken and bruised in more ways than one. I mean, how can a man do this to a child, and how could a mother allow this to happen to her baby girl? I could not understand why this had to happen to me. I mean, was running in the house worth the pain I received? I'd much rather have the whipping or the slap than to have to feel this pain ever again. You would think this was over after I got out of the tub, but no. I was slapped for yelling. I mean, you try to be in that much pain and not scream! My body hurt for days. I didn't realize then that, even beyond the pain, agony, and discomfort he gave me, that man, with the approval of my mother, took something from me I was never going to get back. He took my innocence, even though he wasn't the first to do so. He took my faith: my faith in my mother and my faith in the safety of home. He left me with shattered trust, and so did she. It was around this time that her status changed from Mommy to Lyla. I was so young, but I was old enough to know that mommies don't do this.

Personal Discovery:

Take a deep breath. I recognize that this is a deeply traumatic story, and I'm more than thankful that I'm able to write about it. There are so many horrors to the trauma shared in this story, but I'd like to focus on the fact that it shows how a person, even in early childhood, can lose faith in the protection of a mother (or guardian or anyone that is supposed to be trustworthy). Mommies are supposed to care for you and nurture you and not lead you into the fiery furnace.

1. Think of a time when you trusted someone who was supposed to be trustworthy or protective, but they let you down. How did that experience change your understanding of what protection means?

2. What are some small steps you can take today to rebuild trust in the safe people and places in your life?

3. Trauma in early childhood can make it hard to recognize boundaries, know what's truly safe, or trust even those who've earned it. How have

your childhood traumatic experiences shaped the way you see and respond to life as an adult?

4. My counselors have taught me that the Mommy wounds are some of the deepest to heal. When you begin to recognize how trauma has affected you, how can you offer yourself grace and compassion for where you are right now?

Story 11: The Year of Completion

(Content Warning: This story contains descriptions of sexual abuse and/or violence. Please take care of yourself while reading.)

Age seven seemed like it would never get better. It was abuse after abuse. How much more brokenness can this little body take? I was sent to my room for fighting with the girl next door after she hit me and broke my toy. My punishment: I spent three days in my room with no food or drink, and I had to pee in a bucket. I got whipped each day. All this as punishment for a fight that I didn't start. I never knew why Lyla was so mad at me.

The last day I was in my room, Lyla was in her room. I began to hear a lot of screaming and breaking and slamming. My brother came beating on my door saying, "Open! Please open!" I opened the door. I just knew I was going to get beaten for opening the door, but when my little brother is crying for help, I'll suffer whatever I have to. This time, however, it was not me being hit; it was not me that a man was on top of. It was Lyla. She was the one screaming for help. She was the one saying, "Please stop! My kids are here." She was the one with his hands on her throat, and for a moment, I wanted her to feel that way I felt and hurt in the way I had been hurt. I wanted her broken the way I was broken. But through it all, that was still my mommy, and nobody hurts mommy!

I ran into her room, hitting the man and telling him to get off my mommy. I kept hitting him with anything I could pick up. I'm sure I didn't realize how weak and fragile I was because of the lack of food for three days. I'm sure the adrenaline kicked in, masking the fact that I was in no shape to be trying to fight an adult… besides the fact that I was only seven years old. Sure enough, things started to change when he slapped me so hard that I ran into the dresser. I was hurting badly, but that didn't stop me. I told him to get off my mommy now, or I was calling my granny. Lyla yelled at me, telling me to get out, but I just couldn't. I couldn't walk away knowing Mommy was being hit and hurt. I began hitting him again, this time, I was on the bed hitting him. He then hit me so hard that I flipped off the bed. I was asleep after that, because the next thing I remember is him on top of me with his treasure box in mine. Oh, it hurt so very bad! He was yelling at me, saying, "Go ahead! Hit me now. Go ahead! Say something else." I just cried quietly because I just knew that it hurt so bad, and it would be over if I just didn't fight.

I hated being seven. I hated that people at church talked about it being the year of completion. Not to me! Seven was a year of heartbreak, abuse, excruciating pain, and what seemed like one hit away from death. I never knew Lyla got hit, too. Maybe that's why she hated me so much… because she got hit so badly herself? I thought, "Maybe now that a man has hurt her treasure box, she won't let them hurt mine." Boy, was I wrong!

Personal Discovery:

At the young age of seven, I wanted Lyla to hurt the way she hurt me or caused me to be hurt, yet I felt the need to protect her because I knew that no one was supposed to feel that way. Although I could have and almost did, I didn't get a hard heart to the one who caused me what seemed to be endless suffering.

1. Thinking back to some of the hurts of your past, did they make your heart hard?
2. How have your past pains hardened your heart? Dig deep to identify those experiences and feelings that caused your heart to harden, and then begin to release the hurtful emotions from those painful memories.
3. Have you ever longed for love from someone—maybe a parent, a partner, or anyone—only to be met with rejection or disappointment?
4. In my healing journey, my counselors have encouraged me to love and mother myself. What are some ways you can care for and love yourself that might begin to heal the places where you once felt unloved or unwanted?

Kar'Michay Pope

Story 12: What Goes Up Must Come Down

(Content Warning: This story contains descriptions of sexual abuse and/or violence. Please take care of yourself while reading.)

Reunification happened, and boy, were we excited! My siblings and I were finally back home and together with Lyla... no boyfriends or drugs... nothing was wrong. I mean, everything was absolutely perfect. Well, I should have known that it was just a matter of time before things took a turn for the worse. It seems to really be true: what goes up, must come down. Three months in, and already, men started coming around. One actually lived with us. He tried to play daddy for all of us, but daddies were not supposed to hurt you. Well, maybe they were? I felt as if I couldn't do anything right. I cooked; it wasn't good enough, so a slap was what I got. I cleaned, and wham... a hit was all that I got. And taking care of my siblings... that was not good enough either.

Things began to get rough when Fred, one of the boyfriends, was after my baby sister. That was one of the few times that I stood up for something. He was not about to do something to my little sister! I stood up and I said, "Take me and do whatever you want to me, just please don't touch my sister." He said, "You'll be mine until I'm done with you." I said, "Okay, yes, Sir." That was the first day I was his sex slave. He did whatever he wanted, and no matter how much it hurt, no matter how many times I was hit or choked, I obliged. I lost all sense of myself. I lost who I was. All of my identity was wrapped up in him. He made me feel as if I was a nobody, like I was his property, and truth be told, I was. I belonged to him. He was my master, and I his slave.

I never knew when it was going to stop. I prayed that it would just be over. I prayed to God, "Save me from him. Give me a way out." I even prayed for God to kill me; if this was going to be my life, I didn't want to live it. Lyla became pregnant, and little did we know, she wasn't the only one; I was pregnant as well. So here I am, 12 years old, having a baby. Of course, the child within me had no chance of survival. I was beaten to what seemed to be within inches of my life. He said, "Ain't no way you deserve to carry my baby." After this beating, which caused a miscarriage, I was carried to my room, I'm told, and I slept for what felt like days. I woke up to the realization that my womb was once again empty, and I was numb. I was in so much physical and mental pain, and I had no one to help me. I had no one to hold me and tell me that everything was going to be alright. I was alone in all ways possible.

Soon after that, Fred moved out. I assumed the abuse was over now that he was gone. Nope! A month later, it all started again, except this time it was man after man after man. Drugs became more important than a daughter's body and protection. I endured years of torture before we were once again taken from our home. This time, because she violated her parole. THIS is why we were taken. I mean, I was grateful, but come on! Not because I missed almost a year of school, not because I had constant bruises, not because I became more withdrawn, and not even because they saw the cuts I had placed on my arm from cutting myself. Really? I mean, no one saw the warning signs that I was in agonizing pain. Did anyone even care?

So, it was back to foster care we went. This family was definitely not like the wonderful family I lived with when I was nine. The mother left us with the father all the time. She knew how he looked at me and the other girls. She knew! He became more and more aggressive as time progressed, and then it happened. He began to touch and molest me just like all the other men had. "Not this again, God!" I cried from within. I even prayed for something bad to happen to him. I know, I know, that was evil of me. I just wanted to finally be free. SOMEONE, please see me and set me free!

Personal Discovery:

In this story, I felt hurt, alone, abandoned, and worthless, but I survived. Even in a broken situation, I wasn't broken, though I thought and felt for sure that I was. I'm discovering that feeling alone and abandoned left deep wounds in me in places where I questioned my worth and my belonging. But I'm also learning that my loneliness doesn't define me. Even in the emptiest spaces, I'm finding that I am still valuable, still seen, and still worthy of love.

1. Name a situation from your childhood in which you felt hurt, alone, abandoned, or worthless (or all of the above). Take a few moments to accept and release those feelings (see "Therapeutic Ways to Release").

2. What words of encouragement (not condemnation or judgment) can you give your younger self to begin the healing process?
3. Do you ever blame yourself for the pain you went through? Where does this self-blame come from?
4. What does healing from the pain look like for you?

Story 13: The Fight

I hear my name being called, but I can't seem to bring myself back to reality to answer. My name is called again, and I vaguely remember slowing down enough to figure out why someone was yelling my name so much. When I came to myself, I realized that I was sitting on top of this girl, banging her head against the pavement, not even noticing the blood everywhere. The day had started off much like other days, but a little better than most days. I was 11 years old, and we were outside playing. My siblings and I rarely got to play outside, so it was a real treat.

While we were playing outside, a boy on a bike rode by. I looked at my brother and asked, "Is that the boy you all call One-Eyed Willie?" I wasn't trying to make fun of the boy. I was just asking out of curiosity. Well, the boy hears me and gets angry. He says, "I'm going to get my sister to beat you up". I responded back, "I'm not scared!" knowing good and well I had never been in a fight in my life, and I was indeed a bit scared. Well, he held true to his word. We had gone back to playing; I looked up, and here he comes, marching down the street with his older sister.

She walks right up to me and, without saying a word, pushes me. "Please stop," I said. She pushes me again and says, "Go ahead and make me." I responded, "Please, I don't want to fight." She says, "Well, too bad. No one picks on my brother." So here I am, a scared 11-year-old looking at a girl who was way bigger than me. I turned to walk away, and she pushes me in the back. At that moment, all the times I was hit and couldn't fight back came flooding back to me. I turned around and charged at her. She was in utter shock, so much so that she didn't even fight back.

All I could think of was all the men who hurt me, and I began to hit them back. Finally, I was getting my revenge on them. Finally, I was the one winning. I was in a zone and not realizing that this girl was not any of the men who hurt me. Lyla was called because my brothers couldn't get me off her. She came outside and slapped me back to the present. She yanked me by my arm off the girl and began to beat me in front of everyone who was outside. I didn't understand. I did not start the fight; in fact, I tried my best to walk away. So, why was I now being beaten? When she was finished with me, she helped the girl up and allowed her to hit and kick me. I was later told that I was not to fight, and even if they started it, I was not allowed to fight because I must have done something to deserve it. This was the first and last physical fight I was ever in with a peer, but the fight for my life was far from over.

Personal Discovery:

In this story, I felt like I had to defend myself constantly, and I unconsciously began to defend myself against the many men who had damaged me. For so long, I felt like I had to explain myself, to prove I wasn't who they said I was, to justify my choices, my feelings, even my pain. I defended myself not just with words, but with silence, overthinking, and constantly questioning whether

I was too much or not enough. It came from a place of survival, of wanting to be heard, seen, and understood in a world that often misunderstood and discarded me. Eventually, I began to ask: why do I keep handing out explanations to people who only want to judge, not understand? Why do I feel like I have to earn the right to be me?

What I've discovered as I've begun to heal is that my worth is not up for debate. I no longer owe everyone a version of myself that makes them comfortable. I don't need to shrink, over-explain, or defend my truth to protect people from their own discomfort. The more I trust myself, the less I need to convince others. That doesn't mean I've stopped caring; it means I've started caring more about my peace than their approval. Now, I choose where my energy goes. And sometimes, the strongest thing I can do is stand in quiet confidence, knowing I don't need to defend who I've become.

1. What situations tend to trigger your need to defend yourself?
2. What do you feel in your physical body when you want to defend yourself?
3. Do you often feel like you're being attacked, or just not heard? How do you react in these situations?
4. What are you trying to protect when you defend yourself? Is it your values, your worth, or your truth? What tends to threaten those things, and how can you reclaim your power when that happens?

Story 14: Poolside

(Content Warning: This story contains descriptions of sexual abuse and/or violence. Please take care of yourself while reading.)

It was hot outside and there were no clouds in the sky. The pools were starting to open, and summer was officially beginning. Beautiful days like this took my mind and heart away from all my problems sometimes. So, in my mind, it seemed like this could be the day that I would be freed somehow from all my pain. Of course, I was, once again, wrong. It was quite the opposite. I was 12, and I was anticipating the summer. I'm not quite sure why, though; I just truly believed that this was going to be a great one. Ceci, my friend from the neighborhood, and I were finally able to go to the pool after a long winter and spring. She knocked on the door of my papa and granny's house, where I was staying for a while. Although it wasn't the perfect environment, it was better than staying with Lyla. Anything was, really! Expecting Ceci's arrival, I answered the door. "Come on, we're going to be late!" Ceci said. "Late for what? The pools are open all day," I said with a snicker. I grabbed my towel and swim bag, kissed Papa and Granny, and left the house, walking to the nearby park and community pool. The pool was amazing! Here we were just kids being kids... playing in the water to escape the hot sun. Little did I know that things were about to change for the worse.

We were at the pool for about two hours when I saw him. I knew him, but I couldn't remember how. He kept walking toward us and staring at us. Then he called my name. The way he sounded made me instantly afraid. "How does he know me?" I thought. "Who is he??" I jumped out of the pool and went to him as I was always taught to do with adults. "Why are you out here wearing that?" He spoke. I looked down at my one-piece bathing suit, thinking, "I'm covered completely!" I said, "I thought I had on a lot of clothes." He said, "Does your uncle know that you are out here looking like this?" "Yes, Sir. He knows where I am," I replied. Suddenly, I recognized who he was. It was Larry! I hated Larry! He was one of my uncle's minions. How did he find me? How did he know to come here? Unfortunately, I think it was my uncle who told him to come out to check on me, and that's never a good thing!

Larry told me to meet him at his car because my uncle needed to talk to me. I told Ceci that I would be back. As I walked to the car in ultimate compliance, I was so scared! My uncle knew where I was! Why did he want to see me? What was he going to do to me this time? When we arrived at the car, I realized that it wasn't my uncle who wanted to talk to me. He wasn't even there. Larry told me to get in the car. I obeyed. He said he was going to tell my uncle if he didn't get what he wanted. I was used to those words, so I thought I knew exactly what he wanted. He started kissing me and touching me. He then pulled his pants down and forced my head down on his penis and made me give him a blowjob. As bad as it may sound, I'd rather him just rape me than for him to make me give him a blowjob. A blowjob just seemed extra horrible, maybe because I wasn't used to it. It just degraded me even more than the rapes and beatings. I felt lower than low! Once he finished and he had ejaculated all in my face, he said that I could wipe my face and "get out". I was dejected and humiliated, but that was an order I was glad to obey. I went back to the poolside, and Ceci asked if I was okay. I smiled and said "yes", knowing good and well I was on the verge of a breakdown... once again. I got back in the pool and swam and cried. She never knew it. We finished and walked back to the neighborhood. I went into the house, changed clothes, and slept for the rest of the day. "Will my life get any better?" I thought. "Will this ever end?" I didn't think so. I was sure it wouldn't. If it hadn't gotten any better in all my life, I had little hope that it ever would.

Personal Discovery:

In this story, I was made to do something that was completely humiliating and degrading. It was hard to process the situation. Being humiliated left a mark that I didn't talk about. It wasn't just the moment itself; it was the way it made me feel afterward: small, exposed, and unsure of who I was. I kept wondering what I did to deserve it, replaying the scene in my mind, as if changing something could undo the shame. For a long time, I carried that feeling like it was my fault. I stayed quiet, not because I agreed with what was done, but because I didn't know how to stand up without falling apart.

What I eventually realized through my healing journey was that humiliation thrives in silence, but it doesn't have to live there forever. I started to see that what happened to me was not a reflection of my worth, but of someone else's need to control, belittle, or diminish. I didn't need to fight back loudly to reclaim my power. I just needed to stop believing I had none. Healing didn't come from erasing the experience; it came from understanding that my dignity was never truly taken. It was waiting for me to come back to it.

1. Have you ever been humiliated? If so, how did it make you feel about yourself?
2. How has a disappointing experience affected your self-image or confidence?
3. What beliefs about yourself might be connected to disappointing experiences?
4. What would healing from a humiliating experience look like for you?

Story 15: A Dish or Two

It was in the middle of the night, and all the kids had gone to bed. We were all asleep, and I was awakened out of my sleep. "Get up right now," Granny said. I jumped up quickly with true fear. "Go downstairs right now!" she said. So, down the stairs I ran. She pushed past me into the kitchen, and as we both arrived there, I saw that all the dishes were out of the cabinet, and I was confused. Why was I being called to the kitchen? It was not my dish day. I tried multiple times to tell her it was not my day; however, she did not care. She was dead-set on making me pay for her kitchen not being the way it should be when she got home. As tears rolled down my face, I proceeded to wash and put away dishes. She must have thought that I slammed a dish or two because the next thing I remember was being grabbed by the throat and slammed against the refrigerator. I could not breathe. I was being cussed out, and I really couldn't understand why this was all happening.

She let go of me, slapped me, and told me she would break me if I broke her dishes. I cried and put the dishes up as gently as I could while listening to her on the phone talking about how dumb I was and how she was going to beat my behind after I finished for not doing the dishes right the first time. I finished the kitchen and made my way back up the stairs. When I got upstairs, the girl whose dish day it was, Sarah, was laughing at me. She was a foster child that my Granny was raising. At the time, I was living with Granny, and I had come to realize that Sarah was good for not doing her work and allowing someone else to take the blame for it. So, when I got to the top of the stairs, she was there waiting (and laughing). I pushed her out of my way, and she then slid down halfway on the stairs. It was so loud that Granny yelled up the stairs, asking what was going on. Sarah said that I was mad and pushed her down the stairs for no reason. I said that it was not true. Then, I said that I pushed her because she was laughing, that she got out of cleaning the kitchen when it was her day.

Sarah responded by calling me a liar, and by the time she said I was lying, Granny was up the stairs yelling at me to come here. When I got there, she grabbed me by my arm and slung me against the wall. I kept trying to explain myself; however, the more I tried, the angrier she got, which equals slaps for me. She was so mad she just started wailing on me. When she finished, I was told to go to my bed and not to say, "one more damn word". I did not say anything to anyone for about 3 days, apart from a respectful good morning. I did not understand why my word was never taken to be true. Why was I always in trouble? I was not perfect by any means, but I was not the troubled child that I was made out to be all the time. I guess it was just easier to punish me because I would never talk or fight back; I would just take it. None of it ever made sense, and unfortunately, I will truly never really know!

Personal Discovery:
In this story, I realized that few things broke me like being told I was lying when I was telling the truth. It made

me question everything, my memories, my voice, and even my worth. I learned that being innocent doesn't guarantee you'll be believed or understood, and being disbelieved can feel like losing your voice in a room full of noise. However, over time, I discovered that my truth doesn't need validation to exist. I don't have to prove my worth to those unwilling to see it.

1. Can you recall a time when you were deeply disbelieved? What happened, and who was involved?
2. What emotions did you feel in that moment? How did you respond?
3. How did not being believed affect your sense of self or your confidence in your own experiences?
4. How has the experience of not being believed shaped the way you share your feelings or needs with others now?

Kar'Michay Pope

Story 16: Numb

(Content Warning: This story contains descriptions of sexual abuse and/or violence. Please take care of yourself while reading.)

Age thirteen was one of the worst years of my life. I had started my menstrual cycle at age eight, and it was terrifying because no one told me what to expect or what that meant. Well, for a girl that is being raped often, it means pregnancies. The pregnancies started around age 10, and I was always made to get rid of the babies. Then, at age thirteen, I found myself with child, yet again, by God knows who. I was able, however, to keep the baby this time. I thought I was going to be a mom, so I was sure that things would finally be different… be better. I was wrong, so completely and traumatizingly wrong!

About a month after having my baby, my uncle and his friends were at my house, as they often were. My uncle's friend took my baby from me and took her to the backyard. He had his other friend drag me outside as I screamed for my baby, not knowing what was going to happen. Questions began to swirl in my head like a tornado. Was I going to get beaten again? Is my baby going to be beaten? What did I do so wrong this time? Where was Lyla? Why was she gone and allowing this to happen to her baby girl and grandbaby? Although I expected something bad to happen, I never expected what was about to happen next.

After making it to the backyard, I was made to kiss my baby and tell her goodbye. Then, my baby was placed in a garbage bag. I was so lost. Were they going to throw my baby away? If so, I could go get her back after they left. So, in the midst of all of the chaos, I was hopeful! This was one time in my life when I was actually a bit positive. Yet things were about to get worse... so much worse. My uncle's friend placed the bag with my baby in it on the ground, pulled out a gun, and shot my baby right in front of me. I screamed with a scream of death. "Noooooo!" I yelled. "No, no, no, no, no!" I yelled over and over again. How could they do this to a child who has done nothing wrong? What could she possibly have done to deserve this? "Kill me instead," I yelled. "Why, why?!" I didn't understand, and they never gave a reason other than," This is what you caused; this is what you deserve." "What did I do? What did I do?" I cried, falling to my knees in agony and total despair. In that moment, I began to join them in blaming myself, and they just walked away as if nothing just happened.

I didn't understand. I just didn't understand. Why or how could God allow this to happen to me and my baby? I was so angry at God; if anyone could have and should have stopped this, He should have. I became numb and without feelings, yet so much hurt, agony, and despair overtook me because my heart was genuinely wounded. My heart was broken... crushed... destroyed.

My grief was so intense that I could barely sleep, eat, shower, or cry. I couldn't cry anymore. Six weeks later, my uncle came over with the same friend who shot and killed my baby, and I looked at him with disgust. He told me to shower and go to my room. I just did it. I didn't care. What little fight I may have had was completely depleted. He and his friends did what they wanted as usual and seemed to be upset that I didn't fight back. I was slapped and punched that day, yet I said nothing. I silently cried. I just lay there and cried. When they finished, I got up, took a shower, and lay back down. At this point, I just didn't care what they did to me. I mean, what else could they take from me? What else could they do to take a part of me with them? I thought, "God doesn't care, so why should I?" Numb... I felt so numb. I had no feelings. I cared no more. My anger against God became stronger and stronger. I was convinced that He didn't truly love me; he really didn't care about me. I wrote a letter to God during that time. My letter went something like this:

"Dear God, I served you with all my heart. I loved you more than life itself. I believed you would take care of those who worship you. All of my life... well, the times I can remember... I called you my savior even though my life has been less than great. In fact, it has been horrible. It has been agonizing. I didn't blame you, I believed in you to fix all that was happening to me, so that I could be able to serve you more. I have been broken, battered, and torn over and over again, yet I served you. I have been shattered, beaten, tossed away like I was nothing, and yet I served you. I served you with all that I have been through and all that I have lost or had taken from me. I served you, and you failed me. You left me in the dust. You allowed so many bad things to happen to me, and you did not hear my cries for help. I guess I was not good enough; I guess I was not worthy enough, I was not lovable enough and smart enough for you to care about me. Yet I trusted you, I loved you, I wanted to be all that I could to be, so I could be more like you. What else could I have done to not deserve this? An innocent child died, a young mother's heart was destroyed, and you did absolutely nothing to help. You know everything, and you say everything happens for a reason. So, tell me, God, what was the reason for this?"

This was my letter to God, and it was signed "Your Broken Girl". I didn't know what else to say.

I was truly destroyed, and no one was there to help me. No one was there to help me process my deep pain. So, what did I do? I tried the only thing that was rational in my head: suicide. I downed a bottle of painkillers that were in the house, and I left the house. I didn't want them to say anything to me, even though I knew they wouldn't stop me or even care. I just didn't think they deserved to see my dead body and get the glory of me finally being gone. I made it to the school that was near the house before I collapsed. I don't remember much after that; I just remember seeing the school. This was not my first suicide attempt, but the beginning of a cycle of multiple suicide attempts that went on for many, many years... even after I moved to Huntsville and gained a new life.

I woke up a week later in the hospital, only to realize that I was still alive. I was furious! I was furious at

God once again, saying, "You let my baby die, now you won't even let me die!" When I got out of the hospital, I was released to go into foster care yet again. If this was what my life was going to continue to be like, I didn't want to live it. I became obsessed with attempting suicide. I failed this time, but I was determined that I was going to get it right soon enough. I couldn't imagine any other way to get freedom from my anguish.

Personal Discovery:

In this story, I was completely numb… I just didn't care. I mean, what else could anyone do to me or take from me that was worse than what they had already done? When the trauma happened, something in me shut down. On the outside, I was quiet while on the inside, I was a silent wreck. I told myself I was fine because feeling nothing seemed safer than feeling everything. Numbness became my shield, my way of moving through the world without falling apart. But over time, I realized that numb didn't mean healed—it meant hidden. I was surviving, not living.

The turning point came when I couldn't recognize myself anymore. I missed my own voice, my own emotions, my own sense of being real. "Enough is enough" meant I was done pretending that silence and stillness were the same as peace. It meant giving myself permission to feel again, even if it was messy, even if it hurt. Slowly, I began to reconnect with myself: through tears I thought I couldn't cry, through moments of stillness that didn't feel empty anymore. I'm learning that healing doesn't mean going back to who I was before; it means discovering who I am now, with honesty, courage, and compassion. And that version of me deserves to feel, fully and freely.

1. What is something so traumatic that it's hard to even think about? Now's your chance to write your story. With support around you, write about that trauma and how it affected you.

2. How have you felt abandoned by God amid your pain?

3. What does your letter to God need to address? Write it now, being fully and completely honest. Don't hold back!

4. Are you holding yourself to an unrealistic or unfair standard? What steps can you take to allow yourself to be free?

Kar'Michay Pope

Story 17: The Thief in the Night

(Content Warning: This story contains descriptions of sexual abuse and/or violence. Please take care of yourself while reading.)

It was springtime. I knew this by the crazy amount of pollen that seemed to be in my nose. This spring, I was 14, and it was foster home time again, and, for some reason, I believed wholeheartedly that this time would be different… better. My foster parents seemed to be nice; this fueled my hope to finally have a good experience, a normal life. As I had hoped, things were amazing with this family for the first two months, but then things got pretty bad. I was the only foster child who lived in the home. They had one son as well as two older daughters who had just moved out. The son, my foster brother, became friendly with me. He followed me all around the house as if he were making sure I was doing the right things and behaving. He then began to make little sexual hints and comments… comments that I now know were leading to something much more.

One night, in a bit of a here-we-go-again moment, my foster brother came into my room in the middle of the night. Of course, the room was dark; I had one little nightlight that was barely working. Lying on my back, I could feel him rubbing on me through the blanket. He proceeded to pull the blanket off me and began rubbing all over my body. It felt so weird and so wrong at the same time. He wasn't beating me or forceful, but he wasn't supposed to be in my room, much less rubbing my body. I thought that since he was not being harsh or mean like I was used to, he surely wouldn't do anything more than rub me. I didn't know what to do, so I pretended to be asleep, thinking that if he thought I was asleep, he would just leave. Nope! Once again, I was wrong. In time, he pulled my panties slightly down, climbed on top of me, and inserted himself inside me as if I were a big dog ready to be mounted and conquered... and it was his job to do it. The many years of rapes I had experienced since the age of five taught me to lie there, not say a word, and not fight. So that's what I did... once again. I lay there like a limp noodle, thinking and hoping that this nightmare would be over soon. That seems to be what I always thought: "This will be over soon". But it wasn't. It was never soon enough.

I guess he got tired of me not moving at all, because he began to slap me in the face until I opened my eyes. "Look at me and say you want it," he barked. I've known this drill since I was around 8 years old, so I just repeated what he was telling me to say. I had no idea how to say it the way he wanted, and it wasn't in me to keep trying. When he finally finished, he got off of me and pulled his pants up. He told me to pull the blanket up and go back to sleep. It was strange to me that he didn't say, "Don't tell anyone, "As if he was proud of what he had done... as if he had done it before. Since he didn't tell me not to say anything, I decided to do what I had never done before. I decided to talk to my foster parents about it.

The next morning, my foster mom tried to wake me up, and I wouldn't get up. It took her a while to wake me. I just felt sore (inside and out), and I couldn't move.

When I finally got up, I did it! I told my foster parents what happened the night before. They were silent for a while. My foster dad was the first to speak, and he was the type that, when he spoke, you listened! He was about 6'9" tall and 320 lbs. with bluish green eyes. He had a mustache that he never groomed, so it was overgrown and scary. His first words were, "What were you doing when all this happened?" I responded quietly, "I was in bed asleep." He countered, "If you were asleep, how did you know it was happening?" "Because I could feel it," I uttered. He then asked, "Did you ask him to come into your room? "No, Sir," I responded. "I believe you did," he retorted. He then called my foster brother into the room and asked him what had happened. Of course, my foster brother lied and said, "She asked me to come to her room and make love to her." I immediately spoke up (and that's unusual for me), "That's not true!" My foster mom said angrily, "Don't come to us and tell on people when you asked for something!" I just sat there and started crying. My foster mom slapped me in the face for crying, "Stop all of that!" She followed with, "Now get ready for school and say nothing about it again."

"I mean, are they serious right now??" That's all that I could think. "This 18-year-old boy comes into my room and rapes me, and no one even cares!" He entered my room and had his way three more times until he said that he was tired of me, and I was no longer "tight." I never talked about it again. Why should I? I didn't do any good! I was moved from the home around six months later because they didn't follow all of the necessary guidelines to keep their foster home license. I was happy and relieved to be leaving! However, this memory of The Thief in the Night… one that stole more of my innocence as well as the value of my word… followed me. It haunted me for a long time, like a recurring nightmare. I began to think, "I guess I asked for it." "I must have wanted it to happen; that has to be the reason why it just keeps happening to me." I thought rapes, beatings, and pain were my purpose in life… my calling. My 14-year-old brain just couldn't come up with any other reason for me to continually find myself in the same situation. So many different times, so many different men… yet this time, it was a teenage boy, and I was still to blame.

Personal discovery:

In this story, I was blamed once again for the abuse inflicted upon me. This was a consistent story that seemed to follow me all the time. One of the deepest wounds I carry isn't just what happened to me, it's that I was blamed for it—blamed for what I wore, where I was, how I reacted… blamed for not speaking sooner… blamed for the silence I used to survive. And somehow, the shame of what was done to me became tangled with guilt that was never mine to hold. At first, I believed them. I questioned myself endlessly. Maybe if I had done something differently, it wouldn't have happened. Maybe if I had fought harder or spoken louder, someone would have listened. But blaming myself didn't protect me; it only buried me deeper. What I've finally come to realize is this: I didn't cause what happened to me. I didn't deserve it. And I am not responsible for the actions of someone who chose to violate my body and my trust. Their choices were theirs alone. The blame they tried to place on me doesn't belong to me, and I no longer have to carry it. This discovery has been painful and powerful. Releasing that shame has been one of the hardest parts of healing, but also the most freeing. I am not what was done to me. I am not the lies that were told about me. I am reclaiming my story, my truth, and my voice... one step at a time.

1. Has it ever seemed like your word carried no weight or value? If so, how did that make you feel, and how did it impact you afterwards?

2. What have you been blaming yourself for that you need to let go of?

3. When do you feel the most overwhelmed or triggered, and how do you usually respond? Are there steps you can take to respond differently?

4. Are there any physical sensations or places in your body where you hold your trauma, blame, or shame? Identify ways that you may release the tension in those areas of your body.

Story 18: Lost and Alone

(Content Warning: This story contains descriptions of sexual abuse and/or violence. Please take care of yourself while reading.)

See me, I wish someone would see me. Save me, I wish someone would save me. Help me, I wish someone would help me. All these things I have thought or said. You would think that by age 14, my life would be better. Well, the year started off well. I was in a pretty decent foster home; my foster dad only touched me once. I mean, did I have a sign on me that said, "I'm open for abuse," and sexual abuse at that? Why can't anyone stop this? Why did it seem like no one cared? The more I thought about it, the more I was convinced that no one actually did care. As usual, things started to go downhill when Lyla gained custody of me again.

It was raining that day, storming actually. The social worker picked me up first, then my siblings, and we were dropped off at home. I wanted so badly to be happy to be back home, but I wasn't. I wanted to run as fast as I could, because I knew that staying in that house meant Lyla was going to get back on drugs, and she was going to make me pay for her drugs. I knew she couldn't afford them. The older I got, the more I got used to sleeping with men. It's kind of scary that I even started to enjoy it. Not the rape part, but I grew to enjoy the fact that someone showed me some sort of attention. Someone thought I was worth something. Someone saw me, and with nothing else to hold on to, that was something to me.

I, by now, knew the routine: go into the room, take off your clothes, and lie down… don't scream, and act like you enjoy it. So, I followed the rules, day after day after day. This day, soon after returning home, however, was different. This time, there were several men. It wasn't the first time, so I knew what that meant. So, to the room I went to take off my clothes and lie down. You would think that after all the years, it didn't hurt anymore, that my body was used to it by now. But no. Every time it hurt just as bad as the time before. By the third man, I was no longer able to act as if he were great or act as if I enjoyed it. I just lay there staring at the ceiling fan that seemed to be spinning in slow motion. The sound of the air whipping through the blades, and the sound of the rocking that the ceiling fan made from rotating so fast. The sound was so loud, and everything seemed to be moving in slow motion.

The men were talking to me and to each other, but their voices sounded as if I were hearing them while underwater. My breathing was slow, and I could hear my heart beating as if it were the rhythm of each breath I was taking. With every stroke he puts in me, my body slides up and down the bed, and even that is in slow motion. He slapped me, then punched me, which brought me back into reality. "You're not saying you want me," he said. "Say my name." I didn't even remember what his name was. Was it Mike? No, Mike was yesterday. Was it Chris? No, Chris was the one before him. Slap! I got it again. "What the !$#@& is my name, Brat?!". Was it Thai? Nope? He was grabbing my breast, damaging me from the outside in, and expecting me to think. Ken! It was Ken. It finally came to me. "Ken, Baby, I love you. You are so good. I want more. Give me more," I said. My mind slowly drifted back from reality as tears began to run down my face. I was hit again. "What the !$#@& are you crying for? "Ken said. "It just feels so good, Baby," I spoke. There was never a bigger lie I'd told! It hurt. He inside of me hurt. It really, really hurt!

It's crazy... I felt the very moment life went from him into me. I knew when it happened. Six weeks later, I found myself pregnant. "Not again, not again!" I screamed inside. "Not now!" I made the mistake of telling the school guidance counselor, who told the vice principal, who then called Lyla. Lyla said she knew already, but she didn't. I had my friend's mom take me to Planned Parenthood. Lyla told my uncle. When he came over, he said, "You know what this means, right?" I said, "Please don't hit me," which is quite risky for me to say. Often, I would have been hit for just saying that. "Oh, I'm not going to beat your !$#@& for this one," he said, "I'm taking your stupid !$#@& to the clinic. We're not going through this !$#@& again!" So, here we go again. I was going to the clinic to get rid of yet another baby. I was completely numb, and at this point, I didn't even care anymore. I felt nothing.

The doctor called my name, and into the back I went. It was a two-day process, and I knew the process very well. Usually, I would be crying, but this day, not at all! They gave me an ultrasound and asked if I wanted to see the baby. I said, "No, thank you." My mind was racing, and once again, things were in slow motion. I could hear a fly that was flying by the ultrasound machine, and I could hear the hum of the ultrasound machine. The doctor asked me lots of questions, and my answers were either "I don't know" or "yes, ma'am." It was hard, so very hard for me to resist the urge to just run out of the office. The process started, and I had to come back the next day.

We went home and I lay down. I could hear Lyla ask my uncle if it was taken care of. He said, "Tomorrow it will be ". She replied, "Good because I ain't raising no other !$#@& baby, and she's too stupid to do it. "At this point, I didn't care what she said, I didn't care what he said. I just plain didn't care. I was told to get up and clean the kitchen and bathroom, which, as usual, were already clean. I was in pain, but I did it because I didn't have the strength to fight. "You're moving too slowly," Lyla said. "I got people coming over, and my house better be clean!" Stupidly, I said, "Wow! Is it another man here for me? I just want my body." I didn't think; I just spoke. That remark got me punched in the face, and blood began to run down my face. I just knew my nose was broken yet again. I didn't even cry this time. Did it hurt? Yes, but this time I didn't care. I mean, they were taking my baby yet again! What else can they get from me? What else can they take from me? "Get the !$#@& out of my kitchen, you're getting blood everywhere!" Lyla said. I grabbed an ice pack out of the freezer and walked away. I went into the bathroom and cleaned up, changed my blood-stained shirt, and went back to my room. For a moment, everything about being covered in blood came flooding over me, and I cried. I was just so tired of bleeding. I was tired of seeing blood. I was tired of remembering all the bloody days. I was just plain tired! "I'm not gonna ask God to save me, because, well, I know how that goes," I thought.

The next day, we went back to the clinic, and the process was completed. I'd like to say that I felt something, but no. I felt completely outside of myself, looking at myself. I looked so broken. I could not even recognize that girl lying there. I didn't know who she was or why she looked so defeated. She was lost and alone, and it showed. I kept hearing a voice say, "This is never going to end; it will never be over." My hope was quickly diminishing, and I was starting to believe that inside voice.

Personal Discovery:

In this story, I felt completely lost and alone, abandoned, and broken. There was a time when I couldn't put the pieces of myself back together, because I couldn't even find them. Trauma didn't just hurt me; it shattered me. It left me feeling lost in a world that kept moving as if nothing had happened. I felt alone in rooms full of people, abandoned by those who should have protected me, and broken in ways I didn't know how to explain. I questioned my worth, my strength, even my existence. But somewhere in my healing journey, I realized something: being broken doesn't mean I was beyond repair. Feeling abandoned doesn't mean I didn't deserve love. Being lost doesn't mean I couldn't be found. Healing hasn't been fast or easy, but every time I choose to keep going, I reclaim a part of myself. I may not be who I would have been before the pain began, but I am becoming someone even stronger: someone real, someone whole, someone *alive*.

1. How many times have you felt lost and alone? What were the circumstances around these times, and how have they affected your life?
2. Have you found yourself feeling so defeated that you don't even care? What gave you the strength to carry on beyond those feelings and circumstances?
3. How has abuse affected the way you see and feel about your body?
4. How do you talk to yourself about the abuse that happened to you? Is it kind or critical?

Story 19: Invisible

(Content Warning: This story contains descriptions of sexual abuse and/or violence. Please take care of yourself while reading.)

All I have ever thought was that I was invisible and wanted someone to see me. Well, at least I thought I wanted to be seen. It seemed the more that I hid, the more the wrong people saw me. Well, this day was no different. I was seventeen when he saw me. It was cold that day. I remember it well because I was bundled in my favorite brown scarf and black and brown jacket combo. I was invited to her house. I want to say she was a friend, but really, she was just someone that I knew from around the area, and honestly, she didn't earn the right to be named. She said she was having a small get-together. The get-together was going great. I usually do not go to these types of things, but I decided to get out of the house. It was a small group, so I had no problem thinking I was safe. Her dad was in the other room, so I knew we would be okay. Well, I was very, very wrong.

She started drinking. I should have known to leave then, but peer pressure made me stay. Her dad had no problem with a room full of underage girls drinking, and, in fact, he encouraged it. I, who didn't drink, was trying to stand my ground and say no, but again, peer pressure and not wanting to look like the holier-than-thou girl... I partook. By the third drink, I refused any more. My head was spinning, and the white couch and black pillows seemed to be moving and dancing. Her dad came to check on us and then offered me yet another drink. I, of course, said, "No, thank you." Unpleased with that answer, he turned up the music, grabbed me by my face, and began to pour alcohol down my throat. His daughter saw it and laughed and said, "Get it, Dad."

I cried as tears and alcohol ran down my face. Why was this happening to me? Why was no one helping me? I know someone saw this. This was NOT one of those times I wanted to be invisible. Things seemed to be moving in slow motion. He let me go only for me to fall on the couch. I slid from the arm of the couch to the floor, where I stayed for what seemed like all night. A girl asked me if I was okay, and I couldn't even answer her. The words seemed to be stuck inside my head. Then, he grabbed her and proceeded to fondle her. The only thing his daughter said to him was, "Dad, stop! You're embarrassing me. Take that to the room." She then continued to dance and get high. So, in the room he took that girl.

I absolutely knew how that felt. I knew how it was when no one helped me all too well. I knew that feeling of no one coming to save me. So, I mustered up what little strength and energy I had left. Don't get me wrong, I was in pain from hitting the couch and the floor and from the way he handled me, but I couldn't leave that girl back there, and no one else was doing anything. I made my way down the hallway to the only door that was closed, and I opened it. He was on top of her, trying to pull her clothes off. I ran to the bed! I suppose adrenaline kicked in, because at that time I didn't feel the pain I was in, I felt the pain that she was going to go through if someone didn't step in and save her.

He backhanded me onto the floor, yet that didn't stop me. I got up and started hitting him, yelling for him to get off her. He backhanded me again, and this time it took me longer to get up. Before I could get up, he got off her and started calling me names. He straddled me while I was on the floor and started choking me. I thought surely she was now going to return the favor since I was the one who saved her from him. She didn't! She ran! As I lay there trying so desperately to breathe, the room began spinning, and I was trying my hardest to hit him. Suddenly, I became that same little girl who, years ago, was being choked for trying to save her Mommy, so I just gave up. He let my neck go and grabbed my breasts and began playing with them. I, still in a daze, just lay there. He then grabbed my pants and pulled them down. I just knew what was about to happen, so I didn't fight. Well, I thought I knew. He inserted the bottle from the dresser inside me. The pain was utterly excruciating. I can see the Bath and Body Works perfume bottle in my head even now. Pear Berry. That was the scent; it was a Pear Berry bottle. Somehow, he got a kick out of it. I just cried and counted the number of times he shoved the bottle inside me. It was 37. 37 times. 37strokes of pain. 37 memories. 37 moments I can never get back. He saw me. This time, I wanted so badly to be invisible, but he saw me, and wow, was it painful.

Personal Discovery:

In this story, all I wanted to feel was invisible, yet I was seen. As a child, I learned to disappear, not physically, but emotionally. I became quiet, compliant, invisible. It felt safer to shrink, to vanish into the background, than to risk being seen and hurt again. The abuse taught me that silence was survival. I carried that silence for years, buried under layers of shame that never belonged to me. I told myself it was over, but the fear lingered in my body, my relationships, my sense of self. Then came the moment I couldn't keep running from the truth. "Enough is enough" wasn't just about the past; it was about the way I kept abandoning myself to protect others' comfort. I began to understand that healing doesn't mean pretending it never happened. It means choosing to speak, to feel, to exist fully, even when it's hard. I'm not invisible anymore. My story matters. And I am worthy of safety, love, and a life that is truly mine.

1. Can you recognize how being quiet and unseen protected you or kept you safe in some way?

2. In your past, what has invisibility given you that visibility hasn't?

3. Do you ever disconnect from your body or emotions when you feel overwhelmed or unsafe? If so, write about it.

4. Do you, like me, struggle between wanting to be seen and wanting to be invisible? How do you cope with those moments when being seen feels both comforting and terrifying?

Story 20: The New Normal

(Content Warning: This story contains descriptions of sexual abuse and/or violence. Please take care of yourself while reading.)

Sometimes I sit and wonder if this pain will ever go away. Will this cloud that seems to have followed me all of my life ever go away? I guess only time will tell. Clean white walls, marble countertops, cream colored carpet and tile, and a huge bay window are what greeted me when I turned the key to my brand-new apartment. I was 18, and it had been a few months since I had seen my uncle or any family members. I was starting to get used to my new normal. I was at peace finally. I was enjoying my life. I had decorated my bedroom in burgundy and cream with black-and-white pictures of musical instruments adorning my walls. My bed was once again purchased used; however, with a good wipe down and clean sheets, it seemed brand new again, to me at least. A coffee-colored couch and loveseat matched the carpet so well, and my black and white decorated kitchen seemed as if it came right out of a magazine. This peace, this joy, this new normal... yeah! Oh, how I loved this. My job was going well, and I thought to myself every day that my life was finally on the right track and I was progressing in the way I should have been years ago.

However, just when I thought I was finally living in peace, I received a knock at my door. Thinking it was the neighborhood boy, Timmy, who took out my trash weekly, I grabbed my trash bag and opened the door with excitement. I liked Timmy. Not only was he helping me, but I enjoyed being a blessing to him as well because I made sure that he was paid quite well for his services. But no. It was not Timmy coming to take out my trash; it was my uncle. That's right, the uncle that tormented me for so many years… the uncle that believed he owned me and promised me that I would never get away from him. "Surprise!" he said. My face instantly dropped from pure joy to overwhelming fear as I realized that the man who tortured me most of my life was standing at my door with a smile on his face and some flowers in his hand, which I'm sure he stole from somewhere. "Well, are you going to let your favorite uncle in?" he says, as if it were a question and as if I had a choice. How in the world did he know where I was? This time, I didn't tell my family where I was. I learned that lesson! I told some friends yes, but family? No! I guess you never know who knows who. All I knew at that point was that my new normal was temporary and had come to a screeching halt… again.

I replied, "Yes, Sir, come in." But by the time I was saying "come in," he was already halfway through the door and pushing his way through the door fully. I couldn't get the door closed good enough before he slapped me with the bouquet across my face. "How are you just going to move without permission? How do you think it's OK not to stay in contact with me?" He didn't even give me a chance to answer him. Nothing I said or could have said would have sufficed or made the situation any better. He came over with a motive, and apparently, he was not going to leave until he completed his mission. I knew it was going to be bad, but how bad I never knew or could have prepared for. An unexpected backhand to the face, followed by two more strikes, knocked me to the floor. My beautiful, cream-colored carpet was now splattered with blood that poured from my nose. Two kicks to the side, followed by being dragged down the hall by my hair, was apparently on the schedule for the night. By this time, we got to my room, my clothes were half torn off, my beautiful white blouse was ruined with rips and blood, and my brand-new skirt with buttons on the side was busted open, leaving only my panties. Well, he was a pro at getting them off.

He started kissing me and telling me that I had missed this, that I had missed him, and how he knew that I liked it rough. Honestly, I had almost forgotten that smell of Axe body spray or how harsh his tongue was as it danced to an evil song across my body. I had almost forgotten how it felt when he inserted himself into me like I inserted my key into my door to enter my new apartment. It hurt… terribly… and with every stroke, I felt more and more numb. With each stroke, fewer and fewer tears fell down my face. In my head, there was a battle going on. On one side, I thought, "Fight!" while the other side was saying, "Just wait. It'll be over soon. Fighting will only make things worse." This was a common inner battle I had in these situations. The second voice was right. I knew the consequences of fighting all too well. So, I just lay there. I became numb and lost track of his rhythm.

The pain seemed to only get worse and worse, and just when I thought it was over, he flipped me over and began to insert himself into my anus. Oh, the pain! Oh, the shame! Oh, the humiliation! This was something new. This was a pain and a feeling I had never felt before. My tears seemed to find their way back home. The numbness I felt seemed to wear off, and the battle in my head went silent. Next thing I knew, I was hit in the back of my head for, as he said, getting blood on his penis. When he finally pulled himself out, you would think I felt relief, but no. The pain was all there, lingering and throbbing and reminding me of the horror I had just experienced.

I think he left. I don't know for sure when. What I do know is, just like that, once again, he came in like a thief and stole a part of me without so much as a thank you. My "thank you" was beatings and insults. I couldn't move. Every part of me felt paralyzed in pain. I must have lain there for hours, just broken, battered, and bruised inside and out. I was left destroyed in my body and my spirit. When I was finally able to move, I crawled my way to the bathroom to run myself a bath. It took all the strength I had to crawl into that bath. The water, which should have been soothing and relaxing, burned like fire across my body. I stayed in there as long as I could before dragging my battered body out of the tub. The most I could do was grab a nightgown and crawl into bed. Just as I was finally drifting off to sleep, I heard a knock at my door. Oh God no! No, no, no! This time, I thought to myself, "They will just have to tear the door down." I didn't move. I couldn't move. At this point, I'm starting to wonder if every time I have this great opportunity for a new normal, it will be temporary. Only God knows.

Personal Discovery:

There were times when I didn't just feel hurt, I felt broken. Like something in me had cracked in a way that couldn't be repaired. I looked at other people and wondered how they moved through life so easily while I was just trying to hold myself together. The weight of everything I'd been through sat in my chest like silence too loud to explain. I thought being broken meant I had failed at healing, at coping, at being strong. But over time and with much inner work, I began to understand that brokenness is not the end of the story. It's a moment, not a definition. The pieces I thought were shattered beyond repair were still mine to reclaim, to rearrange, to rebuild. I realized that I didn't need to go back to who I was before everything happened; I could become someone new, someone shaped by the pain but not defined by it. What felt like weakness became a quiet kind of strength. And even in the moments when I still feel undone, I remind myself: I am not broken beyond repair. I am becoming fragile, fierce, and full of worth.

1. What do you believe feeling "broken" says about you?
2. What do you imagine would need to happen for you to feel "whole" again?
3. Is there any part of you that still feels intact, strong, or hopeful? If so, identify that part and describe it.
4. Describe a time when you felt broken and believed you couldn't heal, yet somehow, you began to heal.

Kar'Michay Pope

The

Chrysalis

Psalm 27:5 "For in the day of trouble
he will hide me in his shelter; he will
protect me in his dwelling place and
set me high upon a rock."

Isolation / Breaking / Inner Work
(The breaking that builds you)

The chrysalis is a place of refuge, safe, sealed off from the outside world, yet full of unseen change. Inside the cocoon, everything the caterpillar was begins to break down and reform into something entirely new. This is the stage of deep transformation and sacred discomfort, where growth happens in stillness, and preparation gives birth to promise. In this section, I share the moments in my life where change was stirring beneath the surface. These were times of discomfort, shedding old identities, and reimagining what life could be. Though it wasn't always easy, this was the stage where I began to believe that something better was possible, and that I was becoming strong enough to embrace it.

Story 21: Take Me To The King

It's that time again, my birthday! This time I was able to pick the place I wanted to go. Burger King was my selection. Take me to the king! It was amazing! It was my sixth birthday, and my cake looked like a whopper. My cousins were there... one younger, one older. I had two friends who came. It was the most perfect day ever! I got an Etch-a-Sketch and a Rainbow Barbie doll as birthday gifts. I actually got to take all my gifts home with me; they weren't taken away! For the first time, I was special. It was the first time I felt loved. I was waiting for the other shoe to drop. I was waiting for my whipping when we got home, just for being happy for the day. However, nothing happened! No yelling, no hitting, and no drug use.

Lyla was clean, and it was just us. She said it was us against the world, and for some reason, I truly believed it. Nothing was more important to me than for us to be a family. Nothing was more important to me than to be truly happy, and I was going to soak up every bit of it! I got to play with my brothers. They were kind of jealous because, for their birthday, they chose to have their party in the backyard, as if it was going to be fun. Since, of course, I was a bratty big-little sister, I teased the mess out of them. That, I did get in trouble for! "Stop picking on your brothers," Lyla said, "before I take away those toys!" Seeing as I knew she was serious, because she just doesn't play like that, I quickly stopped and allowed them to play with my Etch-a-Sketch.

"Mommy," I said, "can I sleep with you tonight? I'm scared in my room." I was already anticipating a "no" because we were not allowed in her room, let alone in her bed, but to my utter surprise, this time she said, "Absolutely, and you don't have a reason to be scared. I'll always be there to protect you." She didn't have to tell me twice! I quickly hopped in the bed and prayed she was not going to change her mind, but I dared not ask if she was sure. I snuggled up against her and fell asleep.

I woke up with the anticipation that she was going to be mean and I was going to get in trouble. I was afraid when I woke up to an empty bed, "Oh no! I'm in trouble," I thought. This was not the case. I crawled out of bed and opened the door to the smell of breakfast. My granny and Lyla were in the kitchen cooking. "Go wake up your brothers," Lyla said, and I did just that. I asked if I could help cook the rest of the food or set the table. I was given a chance to cook the eggs and set the table! My birthday weekend was more than I asked for and way better than I expected. I'm so grateful for that time when we were able to truly be a family, and I actually felt loved.

Personal Discovery:

I'm realizing that after living in survival mode for so long, receiving something good can feel unfamiliar or even uncomfortable. But I'm learning that I don't have to sabotage or shrink from the good things anymore. I deserve peace, love, and joy, not because I've been perfect, but because I've survived enough pain to know I'm worthy of better.

1. What emotions come up for you when something good happens? How did you respond to them?
2. What are some specific examples of positive things you've struggled to accept in your life?
3. In what ways have past experiences shaped your ability to receive love, kindness, or success?
4. What would it look like for you to fully accept something good without waiting for it to fall apart?

Story 22: The Perfect Day

To awaken to the smell of Folgers coffee brewing meant the day might just be a great day. Well, if this morning was any indication of how the day was going to go, I was more than okay, which wasn't at all the norm for me. The bright sunshine beamed through my blinds, waking me up. It was about 6:30 AM on a Saturday, and usually we were allowed to stay in bed until at least 9 AM. So, why in the world was I awake? My room was closest to the stairs, so I could smell the aroma of coffee as it pervaded the house, blessing the nostrils and awakening the spirits of even the non-coffee drinkers of the house. "Mmm, coffee! I know that smell," I said to myself as I lay in the bed fully awake. Then it hit me... "Coffee!" I exclaimed internally, "Papa's home!" Yeah, boy, my papa was finally home, and the smell of coffee was my key indicator! You see, Papa worked construction out of town and was often gone, so for him to be home was a true joy for me. He was a good man... one of the few good men that I had ever come in contact with. He never touched me in the wrong places like all of the other men did, never hit me, never called me bad/mean names, never kept food from me. He had kind eyes; he was the first to lead by example, the first to hold out his hand to help, and more importantly, the first man who taught me how to truly love. He was my hero, and to him I could do no wrong.

I grabbed my slippers and ran down the stairs, and he must have known I was coming because he was at the bottom of the stairs with both arms out just to greet me. I fell into his arms of warmth and comfort, and I just melted. "Hi, Papa, I missed you," I said with so much sadness in my voice. "Hey, Baby Girl," he said, "What's wrong? You're sad." I said, "I just really missed you." "Well, Papa is here now, and what are we going to do today?" he replied. I stood up straight like a soldier and said, "First coffee with a splash of milk and two spoons of sugar." He saluted me and said, "Yes, ma'am!" and went on to say, "And for the lady, one bowl of Honey Nut Cheerios and two splashes of milk." "Yes, sir!" I exclaimed. I always got to eat at the bar with him. He liked to stand there, drink his coffee, and complete crossword puzzles in pen. I mean, who does crossword puzzles in pen?! My Papa does! Canton Spiritual videotapes played in the background. They were his favorite gospel group, and he loved watching them as they sang. So, just like two old friends, we sat at the bar: he with his crosswords and me with my comics. These moments of peace and connection with my Papa were ever so precious to this 7-year-old girl who had very few precious moments!

We finished our breakfast and cleaned up the kitchen. I got dressed, and it was off to the race tracks we went. I had no idea why we watched horses run in circles and why in the world people got so excited about it, but hey, as long as I got to go and be with my Papa, I didn't care. There were a couple of other kids who would come to the racetrack with their dad or granddad that I would get to play with and run up and down the bleachers with. We always had money to get a hot dog combo with a soda. For us kids, we felt like we were eating gourmet food.

I played until I was as worn out as the horses. It wasn't often I got the chance to play that much without getting yelled at or in trouble, so I took advantage of the opportunity. When it was time to go, I said goodbye to my friends, and we headed back home. I could always tell if he made money at the racetrack or not, because if he did, I got cheeseburgers from "the hamburger man". They were almost the size of my face! I mean, they were BIG, and man, were they good! I mean good. They made my gourmet hot dog and soda taste like school cafeteria food! Sure enough, this day must have been a good day for Papa, which means it was a good day for me! I got my cheeseburger, we picked up dinner for everyone else at home, and back on the road toward home we went.

When Papa is home, we all sit around the table and eat as a family. I liked that. Granny asked if I had a good day and if I was on my best behavior. I looked at Papa, and he looked back at me and winked as he responded to Granny, "Well, why yes! Yes, we did, and yes, she was." The day ended with me taking a shower and then being tucked into bed by Papa. I hated for this day to end. I just LOVED it when Papa was home, and I HATED it when he wasn't. Every day with Papa is a perfect day, and no matter what we did, as long as we were together, it was a great day. He looked at me as if he were piercing my soul through my eyes. "What's wrong, My Sweet Pooh? I know things aren't always easy when I'm gone, but you know Papa is only a phone call away. I am always here, and you can always talk to me," he said as tears ran down my face. I responded in my soft, sad voice, "It's really bad when you're away." And just as I was getting ready to let him in on how bad it was, Granny came into the room. So, I just sucked it all back in and said, "Life is just no fun when you're gone. Everyone misses you." He forehead kissed me and said, "I miss you too! I'll be home again before you know it." "Because home is where I am," I said, finishing his sentence. He smiled and said, "Yep! And where you are, my heart is!" Everyone in the family hated how strong our bond was and how close we were, but I didn't care. I knew things were going to be bad after he left because of it, but I would willingly take it, because that's how amazing my day was every time I got to spend the day with my Papa, my superhero!

Personal Discovery:

This story is full of positive anticipation. For a long time, I didn't know how to look forward to anything. I was used to expecting the worst, preparing for disappointment, keeping my hopes small and quiet. It felt safer not to expect much at all. But slowly, as I began healing, I noticed something shift… a flicker of excitement, a quiet sense of wonder. I found myself anticipating good things, even if they hadn't arrived yet.

It was unfamiliar at first, this idea that joy might be on the way. That maybe things could turn out better than I expected. That I could hope, not out of desperation, but out of trust… trust in myself, in the process, in the possibility of something beautiful unfolding. Positive anticipation taught me that looking forward doesn't mean ignoring the past—it means believing I'm allowed to feel excitement again. It means I've made space for joy, even while healing, and that is a powerful kind of progress. I'm learning to lean into the light that hasn't fully arrived yet, and to celebrate the strength it takes to hope.

1. What do you feel in your physical body when you're positively anticipating something?
2. What kinds of emotions come up when you're excited about a future event?
3. What kinds of events or experiences tend to spark positive anticipation for you?
4. What positive memory from your childhood stands out as a light in your past?

Kar'Michay Pope

Story 23: Fresh Start

The season was spring, and the weather was sunny with heavy pollen in the air once again. I was fifteen, and this spring, for some reason, I had decided that enough was enough. I was making a decision that my body belonged to me, and it was up to me if I wanted to give it away. Well, all of this sounded like good justification in my head, but what really happened was that I was placed in foster care for what I said to myself was going to be the last time.

This foster home was a two-story house, and I happened to be on the second floor with my window facing the back of the house, right above the pool. There was a waterslide that was just at roof level. There was nothing mean or bad about these foster parents... not yet, anyway... but I didn't want to stick around and find out what they could do to me. I and one of the other foster girls living in the house agreed together to run away, you know, because I was too scared to run on my own. We were going to crawl out my window, walk on the first-floor roof to the water slide at the pool, walk down the slide stairs to the back yard, and escape. However, when the time came and I had crawled out my window, down the water slide stairs, and out the back gate, I realized the other girl was not coming.

I knew I only had a small window of time before I would be seen through the window by our foster mom as she made her nightly rounds in the house. I knew if I stayed there too long, I would be found and be in trouble. So, with much fear, I ran alone. All I had was a small bag of clothes and my purse, which held my weekly $50 allowance. I walked up the street to the Ampm store to get change for the payphone.

Yeah, for those of you who don't know, there were these small booths that had phones in them. You put change in, dial the number, and what do you bet... a phone rings on the other end! It was the middle of the night, but one person that I just knew would be up was my cousin. Well, I called her and, of course, she answered. I began to tell her where I was and that I needed her to please come and get me. Just as I thought she would, she came. Even though I knew she would, in my head I kept saying, "I have not talked to this girl in over two years! Is she really going to help me?" She actually turned out to be a huge blessing.

She lived on the southside, and all Lyla's family lived on the northside. So, I knew that at least for the night, I'd be safe. We talked all night about what was going on with me. She was shocked that I was even alive. I told her about being sold for drugs, all the foster homes, and my uncle and his abuse. I even told her the one thing that I refused to talk about, only because she knew I was pregnant two years ago and asked me what happened. So, yes, I told her that I watched my uncle's friend shoot my newborn baby, and I told her to take that to her grave. After our all-night conversation, she ended up letting me live with her.

Two weeks later, we had a plan. She was going to act as my guardian and move me to a school that was close to her house. Again, she followed through! She helped me do independent studies and finish high school in less than a year. I was finished right before my 16th birthday. She said that after I graduated, she was going to help me get on my feet, and she said she had connections at her job and could help get me on my own. After a while, though, I think she became scared that the longer I stayed with her, the closer I was to being found by the dangerous side of the family, and she didn't want her house and her family put at risk. Well, I can't help but understand that. I mean, I ended up staying with her for almost a year, and this was the first year of my life that I went without any abuse.

She kept her word... again. She got with her connections and got me a new ID. I was able to get a job and get my own place. I had a fresh start! I worked as a secretary in a real estate agency. I got my own apartment. The place wasn't much, but it was mine, and for the first time, I felt really safe. However, this freedom and safety didn't last long. I, in my haphazard happiness, told another cousin where I lived. I thought I could trust her. I thought she was safe, so I told her she could come and visit. I suppose I didn't think about the fact that they were probably looking for me. She, of course, told her mom, who told her sister (my granny), who in turn told my uncle.

So, my peaceful life was short-lived. I came home one day to find him sitting on my couch because, of course, he talked my apartment manager into letting him in. Oh, my goodness! What was I going to do now? He demanded that I sit with him and "talk". His talks always left me in pain... so much pain. Well, nothing had changed. It was a full night of torture, of pure hell. I felt like I was outside of my body, watching my body be physically tormented, and I could see the moment where I gave up and just let go. I do not remember much more of the night after that particular moment. All I know is that I woke up fully dressed, sitting in my car (well, my cousin's car that she gave me to use). I cried. All I could think of was the fact that he, once again, stole my peace, my innocence, and my freedom. Then, in the next minute, I smiled because a voice inside my head said, "At least for a year and a half, I had a taste of freedom. It's never too late to fight again."

It wasn't easy, but I found freedom a few years later, a thousand miles away in Huntsville, AL. And once I became free physically, I began the much harder work of becoming free mentally and emotionally. I thank God for the time that I experienced a taste of what "normal" people feel: a job, a home, conversation, nights free from abuse and beatings and full of rest. That fresh start, though temporary, turned out to be a foreshadowing of the life I would one day live with a new family in a new city.

Personal Discovery:

In this story, I was blessed to get a fresh start. Starting over felt terrifying, like standing at the edge of something I couldn't yet name. But as I took each uncertain step, I realized that a fresh start does not erase the past; it's about refusing to allow the past to define me. I discovered that new beginnings aren't always loud and dramatic; sometimes they come quietly, as a deep breath, a small choice, a whisper that says, "Try again."

1. What fears or doubts do you have about making a change?
2. What does starting fresh mean to you, and what motivates you to seek a fresh start?
3. What are you hoping to leave behind and why?
4. My fresh start didn't last forever, yet I was able to appreciate the time I did have. What are moments of freedom or peace in your story that you can look back on and appreciate?

Story 24: What's In a Name (TPID)

I did not like her, and the truth was I did not have a reason for not liking her, not for real anyway. There was just something about her that I did not like. How can you judge someone merely based on watching a video they're in? Well, yup! I did exactly that, judged her from a video. Let me start from the beginning. As a 17-year-old, I was in a dance ministry in my church and was branching out to find other ministries for some new ideas. I needed a refreshing. I felt like our dance ministry was stagnant, and I needed something that would jumpstart it again — you know, bring some fresh fire back into it. I searched and searched for other dance ministries in the area and came up empty. So, I Googled "dance ministry registries" and a bunch of them showed up. I must have clicked on what seemed like hundreds before I came across one that just jumped out at me. Total Praise in Dance (TPID). I think I liked the name because the name of the group I was over was Worship in Dance (WIND). It seemed like something that I would like, so I clicked on the name, and it took me to their website. I loved everything that I saw on their page, and then I came across their DVD for sale and decided, "You know what? Let me check them out."

The day the DVD arrived was like Christmas to me. I don't know why I was so excited about watching a liturgical dance video, but I was. As I watched, I loved their ministry, their worship, and most importantly, I felt like they were long-lost family that I had just found. Finally, I had something that awakened my spirit and gave me the refreshing that I needed. I think I watched that video about 3 times that day! I felt a connection to these people, and I never knew where it was going to take me. I had all kinds of ideas for my ministry, WIND, and I could not wait to start sharing what I felt God had placed in my spirit for us as a ministry. I started to see dances and choreography in my head. I saw bursts of color that would be moves that we should do. I know it sounds a little crazy when you think of dance moves as bursts of color, but somehow it worked for me, and I was loving every moment of it! When I shared my ideas with the dance team, they were on board and loved the newness that our team was experiencing. It was like a fresh wind, no pun intended, had blown over us, and we were all open to whatever God was going to do and whenever He was ready to do it.

I continued to watch the video every day… literally! I felt like I knew every one of the dancers personally. I was drawn in, and they became a part of me. There was this one girl that I loved, and I kept saying that I wanted to dance just like her. I wanted my ministry to be like hers. This dancer, this video, this group of amazing women were my way of escape from the reality that I was living what felt like every day. I was going through a lot of physical and emotional trauma during that time (what's new?!), so for me to find something that brought me a little joy made a world of difference in my life. On the outside, my world was a hot mess. Shoot, on the inside, I think I was way worse. I was being tormented by my uncle, who would just not leave me alone, no matter what I did to try to get away. Every move I made, it felt like he knew, and it felt like I had only this video... this dance ministry... my self-proclaimed new family to hold on to.

After about a month of watching TPID's video daily and, of course, no change in my consistent trauma, I had finally had enough of my reality of torture and constant pain... pain that I knew would never stop if he and I were both breathing (as you know, it had been going on for many years). Since I do not believe in violence to others, I determined (once again) it was I who had to stop breathing. I decided to end my life yet again. However, I knew that this time would work. I had a plan, I lived alone, so I knew no one would stop me. (Mind you, I did not consider the friend I had that was planning to visit from out of town and who had a key to my house.) So, with my plan in place, I had to tell my new family that I was leaving. They had to know that, though I loved them, I would not be around to see them anymore. I know, crazy, right? This group of people who never knew I even existed had to know a piece of information that did not even affect them. But that was how connected I had become to them, and I know now that it was God who connected my heart and spirit with their ministry. So, I sent an email to them stating that I was going to watch their video one last time before I killed myself. Now that I think about it, that must have been a strange email for a dance ministry to receive out of the blue. Here they were trying to minister to the masses, and here I was telling them I was about to kill myself.

I followed through on my statement to TPID. I watched their video one last time, said goodbye, and proceeded to take a large quantity of pills and alcohol and cut my wrist. I got into bed with my wrist bleeding and closed my eyes. The next thing I remember was waking up to the sound of "Lord You're Holy", a song that I had heard and watched every day on the video that I loved. The name "TPID" rolled off my tongue and out of my mouth like water flowing ever so gently. What was going on? Though I had grown to love the song, why was I hearing it? Why was I uttering the name of the group I loved so much? This is not how things were supposed to go. I was not supposed to wake up, but I did.

I found out later that my friend, who was planning to visit me from out of town, found me in bed and called 911. I was in the hospital for about 2 weeks before I became conscious. She had brought the DVD to the hospital and played it every day that I was unconscious. From our conversations over the past few weeks, she knew how much I loved and watched that video. While I was in the hospital, she also contacted the team, let them know what happened, and let them know that I was alive and going to be alright. So, I watched the video "one last time" and then, 2 weeks later, the first words I spoke were "TPID". I repeated it several times before I was conscious enough to say anything else.

Weeks later, when I was finally able to go home, I had lots of messages from TPID's leader. Remember me saying that I did not like her. Yup! That was her! Even though I loved TPID and their ministry, I didn't like one of the dancers, and it turns out that the one that I did not like was the one who had contacted me multiple times to check on me. I almost did not write back. I did not want her to check on me. I did not like her, so why was she the one who was showing so much care and concern? Why was it not the dancer that I loved and admired and wanted to be like? I mean, I did not hate this other dancer, who happened to be the leader of the ministry, and it was super sweet that she contacted me, but I just felt like she was doing it out of obligation as their leader and not that she cared all that much. Nevertheless, I messaged her back, and although it was not an instant connection, it turned out to be something special about her. I found out that she really had a heart for me, and she did care about me and my well-being.

I began to develop a relationship with her, and I found out that, not only was she not what I thought she was, she was so much more, so much better. She soon became like a sister to me and I called her my Sissy. I loved everything about her. The more we talked, the closer we became, and I started to let her in on some of the things that were going on with me and what led me to want to end my life. She was shocked that I had been going through all of the mistreatment, abuse, hatred, and abandonment for so many years and still found a way to smile through it. Over time, she introduced me to her friend, whom I would soon begin to call my brother, and I started to develop a relationship with him as well. I eventually visited their city, which was over two thousand miles away from mine, and fell in love with it. Imagine! These dancers that I watched every day and had developed a family relationship with in my head... I was about to meet them! When I did, not only was I star-struck, I was also caught off guard by how much they all cared for me. Every one of them was so humble and kind to me.

Remember the dancer that I loved and wanted to be like? Here I was face to face with her, only to find out that she was nothing like I imagined her to be... just like my Sissy was nothing like I imagined her to be. I mean, she was nice and loving and caring like the entire team, just nothing like I had fathomed in my head. Instead, my Sissy was all those things. I realized later that it was not my Sissy that I did not like; it was her confidence that scared me. My Sissy was very confident!

Fast forward several years, I found myself living in that city that I fell in love with, dancing on the same team that I so admired, and living with the girl I once did not like. She went from the girl I didn't like to my "Sissy" to eventually being my legal mommy through adoption, and my "Brother" ended up being my daddy. Looking back, I realize that this time in my life of connecting with TPID was a time that set me up for my change, my rescue, my new beginning! It is amazing how God turns things full circle. He knew what the plan was for me all along. To think that all this started with a Google search, a name that caught my attention, a video that I ordered and watched every day for weeks, and an email from me to my new "family". I never thought buying a DVD would have as much of an impact on my life as it did. What's in a name like TPID? For me, it was life... love... new beginnings! All I know is that I am thankful for TPID. Their ministry, obedience to God, and true love for me saved my life... literally!

Personal Discovery:

In this story, my spirit was hanging on to something greater than me. Sometimes the very thing that tried to destroy me became the doorway to something beautiful I never saw coming. Even in the middle of pain, I discovered purpose. What looked like a break was actually a breakthrough. God took what was meant to harm me (suicide attempt) and used it to build me into someone stronger, wiser, and more alive than ever before.

1. What is one painful experience that, looking back, led to unexpected growth or opportunity in your life?
2. Is there a difficult moment you're still waiting to see the positive outcome from? What would it mean for you to trust the process?
3. What is one negative experience you wouldn't want to repeat, but you also wouldn't erase, because of what it taught you?
4. How did that negative event shape the person you are today?

Story 25: Jeremiah

"**F**or I know the plans I have for you' declares the Lord," Jeremiah 29:11. Ten tiny fingers and ten tiny toes... I don't know how many times I actually counted them, but it was a lot! I was pregnant when I moved out of state. I was on bed rest and was told not to do much. I guess moving to another state was not in the guidelines. With all that I had been through, the stress of my hometown was too much. This was a time in my life when the risk to escape felt better than the risk to remain. Very few friends and family knew I was pregnant, and no one knew that I was pregnant because of yet another rape that I had experienced. So, moving to a new city was my best option. Everything seemed to be going OK with my new surroundings and my pregnancy until I woke up in the middle of the night in severe pain. This had not been the first time I had been pregnant, but it was the first time in a long time I had been this far along. More than that, it was the first time I felt this much pain. I knew something was wrong. I'd never heard of pregnancies being this painful, so I got up and went to the hospital.

I was told that I was in labor and that, with me being only almost 5 months pregnant, they did not expect him to live. So, December 6th, he was born with a hole in his intestines because they had not formed completely. His frail body was too weak to do any type of surgery, so it was a waiting game. I was told that if he made it the first month, they would try surgery to correct the issue. Well, he did! He made it! Nevertheless, the nurses and doctors, though they would attempt surgery, told me that I should not get my hopes up, because the chance of survival was still slim. However, before they were able to do surgery, things took a turn for the worse, and instead of getting better, he got worse.

I was at the hospital every day. I still had to go to work, and it was hard getting back and forth, but my baby was worth every bit of it. The hospital staff was very cold and uninviting, as if they wanted me to leave, but this didn't intimidate me. I was determined to spend as much time as possible with my baby! Because he was so frail, I was not allowed to hold him. The best that I got was to stick my hands through the glass of the incubator with gloves on to touch him. As he lay on his back with tubes and wires all around him, I would gently rub his hands and feet. It was my way of letting him know how much I loved him. I don't know why this brought me so much peace, but it did. I guess I just assumed he was going to get better.

About a week or so after they told me he was far too frail to get surgery, I was able to hold him. I guess I should have known something was wrong then; however, I was just excited to be holding my baby for the very first time in over a month. I only got to hold him for about 30 minutes, but it seemed like just a few short minutes. Whatever it was, I was happy to take it. Holding my baby meant the world to me. Another week had passed, and it was nearing the end of the month. "He's going to be just fine." I thought. Then I got the news from the doctor that he was not going to survive. I was furious! I went off on the doctor, screaming, "No! You are not doing your job!" and telling him that he needed to be trying to save Jeremiah instead of just giving up on him. I cried and cried and cried! You see, Jeremiah was a glimmer of hope for me. In all of my years of abuse and hatred and mistreatment, I finally had someone that I could safely love and that could love me. I finally had someone to live for. I finally had hope. When that doctor told me that Jeremiah was not going to make it, it took away what itty bitty hope I felt like I ever had. I felt like I had no one but Jeremiah. And even though he was conceived from one of my many horrible experiences, he was mine and no one could take that away from me... until the doctor gave me this heartbreaking news.

The doctor was so loving, calm, and patient. He said he was there to help me and told me that they were doing everything they could to save him, but he had lived for longer than he was expected to live. That night, I cried out to God. I asked Him to please allow my baby to live; I begged Him! I told Him that I would be a good mom, that I would teach Jeremiah to serve Him. I cried with the cry of a destitute, hopeless, broken-hearted mom. "Please, God save my baby," and "please don't make him suffer the way he is suffering". I was up all night, just on my face before God. I just knew that all was going to be well. I had that, as they say, "faith of a mustard seed". I was not going out without fighting for my son. I stayed in the hospital pleading the blood of Jesus over Jeremiah, the nurse, and the doctors. I was determined to keep Satan from taking my son.

I told the doctors to run the test over, that they had things all wrong. I think they were hurt because I was hurting, which speaks to how kind and compassionate they were. Someone came into the room and asked if they could pray with and for me. I said, "Yes, thanks!" After she prayed, I felt peace, and I was sure that this peace was the sign that I was going to see my baby, but a few hours later, I held him as he took his final breath. On January 22, I watched my baby leave this earth. I cried so hard. I said, "God, you gave me peace. You made me feel as if he was going to live, but you still took him!" Believe it or not, even though I was angry at God and fussing at Him, that same peace came over me again. Then I heard a still, small voice say, "For I know the plans I have for you."

I realized at that moment that God had everything working the way He wanted it to work. Was I devastated? Absolutely! Did I cry every day? You better believe it… for months and years to come! However, what I know now that I didn't know then is that in his short life, Jeremiah made me a better person. This small infant that I could barely hold had changed me in a way I could not even fathom. He showed me what love was when no one in my family had done so. He helped me see the power of my voice because I sang to him daily, and I could tell that it changed the atmosphere. He showed me light when all I could see before was darkness. I am forever grateful for Jeremiah Isaiah. I do what I do now because of him. My hope is that he can look down and be proud that I was his mother. Even years later, I miss him dearly. I celebrate his birthday every year in December, and I remember his death every year in January. I love my Miah Man! Nevertheless, what gives me great joy is the knowledge that I will see him again. Rest easy, baby boy!

Personal Discovery:

Matthew 24:35 says, "Heaven and earth will pass away, but my words will never pass away." I discovered that when everything around me was crumbling and I had no strength left to stand, holding on to God wasn't just an act of faith; it was survival. In the silence, in the storm, and in the sorrow, I found that God was the only constant. Even when I couldn't feel Him, He was holding me. And in that place of deep pain, I learned that His presence was more powerful than any answer I thought I needed.

1. Name a time in your life when you needed to hold on to God's word or His peace when it seemed like what mattered to you the most was passing away.
2. What can you learn from that time?
3. What do you think God was up to?
4. Is it still hard to believe that God was working for your good? How might you grow to trust His goodness, even in the midst of trouble?

Story 26: Run

It was really late at night. I had just gotten into a huge fight with my uncle, and he was ticked off because I was, in his words, "acting too grown, showing your behind and acting as if you don't know who you answer to". All of this because I didn't answer the phone when I was with a few friends earlier that night. Truth is, I didn't hear it, nor was I even trying to keep up with it that night. I just plain didn't care. When I got back to Granny's house, he was there, and that's where the fighting started.

I got out of the car and walked into the front door of my granny's house. A friend was with me, and I told her to wait outside in the car. I walked in the house, turned the corner, and there he was, virtually steaming with anger. I, not even realizing that something was wrong and that his problem was with me, said, "Hello," and proceeded to jog up the stairs as usual. When I heard my name being called and the way it was being called, I froze in my tracks. "Yes, sir," I responded. "Bring your a** back down here!" I heard. I did just that, and it was at that very moment that I realized something was wrong, and this won't go well.

I counted the steps all the way back down. One, two, three, four... when I got to the bottom, I had counted 10 steps and had experienced 10 seconds of dreadful fear for what was to come. When I got down the stairs, he asked me where I had been and why in the world I had not answered my !$#@& phone. I said, "I was with Jessica and Tanya at their house, and I did not hear my phone." This was not acceptable for him. He said, "You should always be by your phone, you should always answer the phone when I call!" I was thinking, "What makes you so special that I need to answer when you call?" However, this was something that I dared not say! I guess I had the look of what I was thinking on my face, because he asked me if I had something smart, I wanted to say. I innocently replied, "No, Sir."

He quickly got up from his seat, grabbed me by my arm, and flung me against the wall. I said, "I'm sorry that I didn't answer my phone. I was not trying to ignore you," when truth was, I really didn't care if he called or not. I, at that point, was just tired of being controlled by him. However, at that moment, I was starting to regret that choice. He slapped me across the face and said, "I bet you're gonna answer the phone next time, aren't you?" "Yes, I will," I promised him. He let me go and told me to go wait in the car for him. By this time, my friend had left. I'm not sure if he told her to leave, or if she heard him hurting me and ran. Either way, instead of going to his car, I grabbed my phone and walked down the street. I called my Sissy in Alabama to tell her what was going on and ask her what I should do. All I ever knew to do was what he told me. Walking away like that was a bold move, and I had no idea what the next move should be. When I talked to her, she told me to go to the police station. There was a satellite police station not far from the house, so I walked to the police station and walked in.

As I entered the police station, a "safe" place, I hung up with my Sissy and talked to two officers. I told them that I was unsafe, that my uncle had hit me, and that he was going to kill me if he found me there. One of the officers told the other officer that he understood what was going on better and that he would handle it alone. They kind of talked back and forth, and the officer who said he would handle it looked a little suspicious to me, so I told him that was okay and that I was fine and walked out of the station. I know this might seem crazy, but my uncle had friends in the police department, which is one reason he was able to do what he did to me for so many years. The way that officer was talking, I didn't trust that he wouldn't just put me in a police car and take me right back to my uncle. It wouldn't be the first time, if he did!

At this point, I was, once again, alone. I just started walking. I had no idea where I was going; I just knew I couldn't stay there. As I was walking, I saw a van coming closer to me. I didn't recognize the van, so I wasn't really too worried. But as it got closer, someone rolled down the window, and I recognized him. It was one of the evil friends of my uncle, and at that moment, I knew I was in trouble. There was no reason to run, because I knew I wouldn't get anywhere. So, I got in and they took me back to the house where my uncle was waiting for me. I guess I should have just stayed with the police officer; maybe the ride back would have been more fun.

Arriving at the house, I was snatched out of the van by my uncle. He yelled at me, "This is your problem! You don't listen! When I tell you to do something, that's what I mean for you to do. Now you know you made it worse for yourself. We're leaving." "Can we just talk for a second?" I pleaded. He snarled back, "Naw, Ain't nothing left to talk about." It was four of us: my uncle, James, me, and Big Ed in an old, dusty-feeling, black van with a grey stripe. It smelled like weed and cigarettes. We stopped by my uncle's house. I thought we were going to stay there, but no. He just went in for a minute or so to grab a few things. I made the mistake of asking where we were going, and I was backhanded in the face. "!$#@&, shut up! You ask too many questions," he said.

We drove for a while before we stopped for gas. I was hungry and thirsty, but I did not ask him for anything. So back on the road we went... where we were going, I didn't know. My uncle had taken my phone, so I couldn't even contact my Sissy to tell her what was going on, get her help, hear her voice, anything. I was again alone and the only female in a van of rapists and criminals, the chief of whom was my uncle. I was raped along this journey more than once. I was so, so very tired, mentally, emotionally, and physically. I was scared to fall asleep, in fear I would wake up with yet another man on top of me and in me. However, I was so tired that I fell asleep. When I woke up again, we were finally at our destination: a house that I was unfamiliar with. I was told to "just get out".

There were lots of people in this house, and they were all getting high and drunk. The house was small and dark. The room that I was told to stay in was in the back of the house and had red colored walls. At least they looked red. It could have been from the floor lamp, which was covered up by a thin red sheet. Besides the floor lamp and red sheet, there was a mattress on the floor. That's really all that I remember from this room that became my home for about three days. I was raped multiple times that night, and there was not a day that I was there that I wasn't raped and that I didn't see multiple other girls being raped.

I was allowed to have my phone at times, and whenever I could, I would contact my Sissy and let her know that I was alive. I always told her that I was OK, even though I really wasn't. She contacted me back, telling me that she had been praying for me and that she had contacted the police, trying to find me. My uncle's friend, who would often take my phone from me and read it to make sure I wasn't doing anything "wrong", saw the message from her. He sent her a message back, as if he were me, saying, "THIS IS MEME YOUR SIS I IN RENO AND IS FINE AINT NO NEED 4 DA PO-PO SHE FINE IF YOU WANT 2 TALK 2 ME FINE BUT WILL NOT ANSER ANY THANG CAUSE I JUST FINE". Of course, you know that my Sissy knew that I didn't write this. Who in the world writes like this? Plus, he called her by her name, which I NEVER do. That's my Sissy! All this did was make her pray harder!

On the third night, a girl that I had never seen before gave me my clothes and said, "Put your clothes on and run". I told her "NO!" and that she was trying to get me killed. She said, "No, I'm telling you, get your clothes and RUN right now". She said it so emphatically, like I couldn't say no or use my own rationale to refute it. So, with much hesitation and fear, I got dressed and ran. This was hard because not only was I overweight, but I also didn't know where I was going. Heck, I didn't know where I was! I didn't know if I would find help or if they would find me first and make me pay for trying to run away. On top of all of that, I had asthma. Yet, I was running. I just ran in the direction that she pointed.

I came to a gas station-type truck stop. A man was pumping gas, and a woman, whom I later found out was his wife, was walking out of the store. I ran up to her and asked if I could use her phone. All I could think was, "I've got to call my Sissy!" She kind of looked at me like I was crazy. I can only imagine what I looked like after I just ran for God knows how long, from God knows where, with my asthma that's God knows how bad. Here I am, a black girl who looked an absolute mess, asking this white lady if I can use her phone. She says, "Do you need help?" I said again in a panic, knowing that my uncle could drive by and see me at any moment, "Ma'am, may I PLEASE use your phone, I just need to make a phone call?" She again said, "Do you need help, Sweetheart?" As I was, in desperation, getting ready to ask her again to use her phone (because my brain just couldn't put together any other words to say), her husband, still pumping gas, spoke up from across the gas aisle, and said to her, "Hun, I think I remember her. In fact, I know I do. She was the coffee girl from Petro… the one that always made my coffee really well." The lady replied to her husband, "Oh yeah, you told me about her!"

She never let me use her phone, but she did ask me where I was going. I responded with my hometown, and she said that they were going to the same place and that they would take me and drop me off. So, with much hesitation and loads of fear, I got in the truck. I was so terrified to get in, and I, yet again, didn't want to fall asleep because I didn't know if I was truly safe. Nevertheless, this couple did as promised and took me back to my hometown. On the way, the wife, Amber, allowed me to charge my phone, and I called my Sissy. I knew she was concerned about me, and even though she was a thousand miles away in Alabama, she was the first person I wanted to contact for help. Of course, my Sissy had lots of questions, trying to figure out if I was TRULY safe with this lady and if I would be safe when I got back home. She told me that I really didn't need to go anywhere where my family could find me. If they could find me, my uncle could find me.

Overhearing my part of the conversation with my Sissy, I think Amber quickly figured out that I was in some real trouble. She asked, "Are you in trouble?" "Do I need to call someone for you?" "Should I take you to the police?" I reacted strongly when she mentioned the police, saying, "NO! Definitely don't call the police, and there is no one else to call." I had no clothes other than what I was wearing, no money, no food, and no place to go. I didn't tell Amber all of this, but I'm sure she could tell, because before we made it to town, she did the unthinkable. She offered for me to stay in their home until I found somewhere safe to go. Not only did Amber and her husband allow me to stay in their home, but they also had their daughter, who lived in the same neighborhood as them, buy me clothes and stay with me because they had to get back on the road in their 18-wheeler.

I look back, knowing that in the midst of a kidnapping, multiple rapes, and a literal hopeless situation, there were angels sent by God to be at the right place at the right time: the lady who told me to put my clothes on and run, the lady and her husband at the gas station, and, of course, my Sissy. It pays to always treat people with love and respect. If I were not the nice, loving girl that Amber's husband remembered from a Petro Truck stop that I worked at over a year prior, I would not have been taken into their truck... much less their home... and given a chance to be free once again. I talked to my Sissy almost daily when I was staying at Amber's house, and I stayed there for two weeks. I left Amber's house to begin my next journey, my new beginning, my new life, and my fear-to-faith leap (see "Story 27: From Fear to Faith") Little did I know that the horrific 3-day experience of being kidnapped and held in a strange place would be the last time my uncle would hit me or rape me. So, you see, every time I think the Lord has given up on me, he shows me that he cares so much more for me than I realize.

Personal Discovery:

In this story, all hope was gone. I had no faith that I was ever going to get out of this situation. I was going to either die or be held forever, was my belief. However, God had something unexpected for me... a blessing in disguise. There were times in my life when I couldn't see anything good ahead. I was too focused on what I had lost, on what had broken me, or on the weight I was carrying just to make it through the day. I didn't expect anything beautiful to come from the chaos. But then something small happened, a kind word, a stranger's kindness, a moment of peace that I didn't see coming. And I realized not all blessings arrive with fanfare. Some show up in whispers, in unlikely people, in the quiet strength I didn't know I had.

These unexpected blessings reminded me that life isn't just about the pain we endure; it's also about the light that still finds a way in. I began to notice things I had overlooked: resilience growing where I thought nothing could survive, joy in places I assumed were too empty to hold it. I learned that even in my hardest seasons, grace was still present—sometimes subtle, but always real. I may not have gotten what I wanted, but I'm starting to see I've been given what I need to grow, to heal, and to begin again.

1. Has God ever worked out what seemed impossible for you?
2. How has your faith manifested in the midst of your fear? Give yourself credit even when you don't feel like you're full of faith (like when I ran).
3. Has your faith ever felt like a source of pressure instead of peace? If so, how did you deal with it?
4. In what area have you had to activate your faith to make it through?

Story 27: From Fear to Faith

It was a day like no other! "A ticket is waiting at the airport for you," was all that was said by my then sister, whom I affectionately called "Sissy". She knew just what to say to get me to the airport. It was scary to leave everything I had ever known, as bad as it was, to go thousands of miles away to a place of uncertainty. "Will they really like me once I get there?" "Will they really regret bringing me there?" These were the questions that were swirling around in my head; however, with both fear and excitement I, with only a few hours to get myself together, got on a redeye flight to Huntsville, Alabama. There was no turning back now! I was on a plane, but trust me when I say... I was not aware of the adventure my life was about to take.

My first layover was in Las Vegas, and I'm not gonna lie... I thought about running then, but I stayed. Leaving now would only feed into the fear that I was so desperately trying to let go of. So, they called my flight, and there I was, ready to board. All I could think was, "OMG! I'm really doing this!" My second layover was in South Carolina. My heart sank into a sea of fear and pain because it was way too late to turn around, and I had left everyone and everything without even a goodbye. So many people counted on me, and what if they fell apart because I wasn't there to save them? I was hurting them; I just knew it! "Why am I doing this?" I asked myself over and over. My peace was nothing if that meant they would somehow be hurt, but like I said, it's too late to turn back now, so I have to keep fighting for freedom for myself.

I couldn't sleep on the flight from South Carolina to Huntsville. I was shaking, my heart was beating fast, I was sweating, I was having a panic attack before I even knew what that was. "Welcome to Huntsville!" the flight attendant said. No way! I wasn't ready! "I'm not ready to get off the plane", was what I told the flight attendant. She looked at me with a sweet, calm voice and said, "Sweetie, welcome home." I mean, how did she know I was here to stay?? I could've just been visiting! I said, "Thanks," and made my way off the plane. With some of my panic subsiding, I stopped on the bridge to take a picture; I guess I just wanted to capture my walk into true freedom... or maybe I wanted to capture my walk into my new beginning. Whatever it was, I, at that moment, was happy to be doing it. I was moving from fear to faith.

"Welcome to Huntsville, The Rocket City" was the other sign I took a picture of. It became like a new adventure, and I was eager and ready to explore it. I got off the plane with one tiny suitcase filled with scraps of stuff I could put together in the short time I had to grab some things and flee the city. I made my way downstairs and outside only to see a bouncing, happy woman. "Sister!!" is all she said at first. "I'm so glad you're here" was next, followed by "Let's go eat!"

I couldn't believe it! I was really in Huntsville, Alabama, and I was with my Sissy, and I was STAYING. Shock and amazement overtook me. If this was a start to what my life in this new land was going to be like, I was thinking, "Why didn't I do this a long time ago?" I often say that if I had to go through all that I went through to end up where I am now, I would totally do it. Well, that was just the beginning of a journey that I had no idea I was going to go on! Would I like it? Would I want to run away from it? Whatever the case, I was blindly going at it. I had to walk by faith and not by sight, because leaving everything I had ever known for something I had never experienced scared the mess out of me. However, I just had to hold on to the One who knew it all and allow Him to guide me. Trust me, that's not easy when you struggle to even trust Him. I knew this wasn't going to be easy; I just never expected it to be so hard.

Personal Discovery:

In this story, I had to truly rely on faith, because fear was crippling. I have come to understand that fear often arises when I try to control what I was never meant to control. It paralyzes my spirit, narrows my vision, and keeps me anchored in doubt. However, in learning to let go and trust what I cannot see, I've discovered faith, not as a blind leap, but as a conscious decision to believe that there is purpose in uncertainty and strength in the surrender. Moving from fear to faith has not been a single moment, but a continual choice to believe that even when I don't know the way, I am still being guided.

1. What has been your fear-to-faith moment?
2. How has fear influenced your decisions or actions in the past?

3. How has faith played a role in your life, and can you identify a time when you allowed your faith to be stronger than your fear?
4. What would faith look like in a situation where you are currently experiencing fear?

Story 28: In the Club

(Content Warning: This story contains descriptions of sexual abuse and/or violence. Please take care of yourself while reading.)

The old saying of "what goes on in this house, stays in this house" can be applied behind any set of four walls. In this case, it is "whatever happens in this club, stays in this club". Those same four club walls that protected so many failed me in all ways possible. The narrative was that I was the bad one, that I ruined people's lives. No one cared to know how I was doing or how my life was damaged and forever changed. I started working at the club as a favor to a church member, and this church member became my boss. It was an amazing job. I had once again found myself in a teaching position, and I loved every minute of it. At the time, I was 32 and working on my master's in social work, and this was the job that made me rethink my college major and lifelong dream to be a social worker. I felt so comfortable teaching and was willing to admit that I was good at it. I was great at it!

Things started to go downhill around June, during the summer all-day sessions, when comments made in a sexual manner began to occur. I played them off as joking and playful. I did not like them or want them, but I could not imagine my boss and fellow church member being serious about these comments. That never even crossed my mind. I would get random calls to the office, and with the door closed, I would be told that I was safe, and I could always come to him and talk. He knew about my abusive history, and as I look back now, he preyed on it. I was told not to worry because I had someone to talk to about my feelings, inside of work or outside of work. These office visits became increasingly personal and inappropriate, having nothing to do with work. I told him how unacceptable his comments were because he was married, not even thinking about the fact that he was my boss, and we were at work.

One day, as usual, I was called into his office. This time, it was to work on something on his computer. He always had an excuse to call me into his office. I was working on his computer, trying to figure out what he needed and then, out of nowhere, I turned around and there it was, his penis, was right in my face, almost touching as I was sitting there, and he was standing over me. He told me to suck it. He said it in a way that made me fearful of him. I did not know this characteristic of him, but all of a sudden, he turned into the many, many men that I experienced all my life. He was no longer a coworker I could trust; he was a male abuser who would hurt me terribly if I didn't do what he wanted, and I had no idea what he was truly capable of. So, there I was in my boss's office, with his genitals in my mouth in straight fear of what was to come. Once it all hit me, I jerked back. I did not want this at all! My pulling back angered him. He told me I could lose everything if I did not do what he wanted. So now, in fear of my job, reputation, and safety, I obliged. This started several months of sexual encounters in his office both vaginally and orally, plus he continued with many sexual comments and conversations. He made these comments when no one was around, both at the club and at church. Once again, I was being coerced/forced to engage in sexual activity. Once again, I was convinced that this lifestyle was my destiny. I mean, why does it keep happening to me?

There were times he would tell me to send him pictures and videos of me. This took me back to my days of being "owned" by my uncle and his friends. When they asked me to do something, I did it. So again, out of the fear that I knew oh so well from my previous experiences, I obliged and sent pictures and video. Then the encounters moved from the office to a hotel. One day, he told me that I needed to pick up my parents from the airport. It was not true. I knew something was not right about what he was saying. I tried not to go. I made excuses about not needing to go, and he argued with them. I was so afraid of what he would do to me. Out of sheer fear, I left the job, got in my car, and started driving to the airport. I did not realize it, but he had left before me. He called me on my personal phone and told me he just wanted to talk and that I needed to listen to and follow him.

Once again, I did just what he said. I followed him. And where did he go? He went to a hotel. I have been raped many times, all my life really, but never from my boss… never from a church member that I trusted… never like this. I felt stuck. I absolutely loved the job, and my reputation has always been of utmost importance to me. I could not imagine my reputation being ruined or losing my job. I just did not know how to get out of this situation or if I ever would. There were many days at the club that I tried to go on field trips to get away from him. Eventually, I gained enough strength to tell one of my coworkers, along with my mom, but I would not let them do anything.

However, telling my coworkers was a huge mistake. They just went back and told him what I said. This only made it worse because he threatened me more and told me that I would lose everything if I said anything else.

I became pregnant by him twice: once without telling anyone which led to a miscarriage, while the other time came as a shock. I was having stomach pain, went to the hospital, and learned that I was pregnant. As if the pain and abuse of my experiences with him were not enough, I had to experience the physical and emotional pain of two miscarriages also. Meanwhile, the abuse stopped briefly as his divorce became final, then he started with the abuse again. The job that I loved so much became a breeding ground for fear, pain, humiliation, entrapment, confusion, and powerlessness. Why was this happening to me again? I often wondered if I had a sign hanging on me that said that I am open to abuse. Whatever it was, I lived in pure fear every day going to work in the club. What was once the best job quickly became the worst job I've ever had.

Personal Discovery:

I am beginning to understand how deeply fear controlled me in this story. It was not just fear of the person who was hurting me, it was fear of being alone, and fear of not being believed. That fear became so familiar that I confused it with safety. I stayed there in that place because a part of me thought I had no other option, or that I somehow deserved it. Looking back, I see how that fear silenced me, paralyzed me, and kept me in survival mode, much like when I was growing up. I was doing everything

I could to make it through while continuing to work and act like all was well; that fear swallowed me whole. Fear completely convinced me that I was powerless, worthless, and stuck. Now I look back and see it was he who was powerless and full of fear. It is crazy how fear can have so much power over you that you forget you never lost it. I now know that abusive behavior is often driven by one's own insecurity, need for control, or fear of being exposed, rejected, or powerless themselves. People who manipulate, intimidate, or abuse others often act out of fear—fear of losing control, fear of inadequacy, or fear of vulnerability. If I knew then what I know now!

1. How has fear kept you in places, relationships, or situations that were hurtful or unhealthy for you?
2. What helps you stay present when fear wants to pull you back into the past?
3. What would you say to the version of you who was doing their best to survive?
4. What does it look like for you to overcome fear and truly heal from it, rather than succumb to it or avoid it?

Kar'Michay Pope

Story 29: A Dream or a Vision

(Content Warning: This story contains descriptions of sexual abuse and/or violence. Please take care of yourself while reading.)

I was being beaten by fists of pure evil and anger, only this time, I felt numb to the pain. I was standing over my body watching as if I were an outsider watching a horror movie, and I could not even turn away. The room was poorly lit, but that did not stop me from seeing the shattered mirror barely hanging on the wall, or the ripped curtains hanging above the window. It was me and him, only I could not see his face. Who was this man on top of me... and why was I being beaten this time? I watched as my body took hit after hit without fighting back in return, yet still it continued. I became unrecognizable. "Who is this child lying there in a pool of her own blood?" I thought. "Is she dead or alive?" I had no idea, and I could not help. I stood there stiff without movement. I watched this man leave, then I watched him return. He stood there as if he were in awe of his handiwork, as if he were proud of what he had done.

I watched as he climbed on top and inserted himself, and for the first time, I felt something. It felt like fire penetrating my insides. Yet I still stood there unable to move... feeling the pain and not even being able to stop it. Finally, sound came back to my lungs, and I screamed a gut-wrenching scream, yet my scream was not heard. Suddenly, I return to my body, only to feel the weight of his body, the sweat as it dripped on me, and the fire my insides were feeling. I could smell him; he smelled like outside, that slightly musty, earthy odor that oozes from your body when you have been outside. That, mixed with sweat, is a smell I will not forget for a long time, forever.

What was happening? What did I do wrong this time? When he finished, he fell on top of me, and the weight of his body made it hard to breathe. I so eagerly wanted to know who this man was. Where was Mom? Why was the house so quiet? Soon he rolled off me and lay in the bed next to me. Everything hurt. Why was he still lying there? They always leave when they finish. Not him, he just lay there. I can still hear his breath as he exhaled and inhaled. Then he spoke and I knew that voice, but not seeing his face made it hard for me to really know.

He told me that I ran my mouth and that I got him in trouble. He said, "I should kill you," but followed that with, "but you're not worth it." As I lay there, tears streamed down my face. My silent tears were caught by my blood-stained pillow. Once again, not only was my body broken, but my soul was also. I turned my head towards him and whispered, "I'm sorry." He turned his head and looked at me and said, "You will be." Then, I saw his face. It was Hank, my boss at the club. As soon as I saw him, I woke up. I was drenched in sweat, and my tears were uncontrollable. I could not believe that this was a dream! Why was my body in pain? Why can I feel the pain as if it happened in real life? I could not move. I was lying in my dark bedroom, and I was shaking in fear. I honestly couldn't tell at the time if it was a dream or a vision. Was it not enough for him to hurt me the way he did? Why does he have to haunt my dreams as well? It feels like sleep is no longer my friend; it has become another one of my enemies.

Personal Discovery

Nightmares bring a new wave of torment long after trauma has supposedly ended. Because of my severe PTSD, I experienced intense nightmares for years. It was traumatizing and demoralizing, making me believe I might never escape the grip of trauma.

1. What are your first thoughts or feelings when waking up after a nightmare?
2. Have you had any recent traumatic experiences or unresolved conflicts that might relate to a recent nightmare?
3. What do you think nightmares are trying to tell you about your current emotional state or mental health?
4. What techniques might help you feel safer or more grounded after a nightmare?

Butterfly

2 Corinthians 5:17: "Therefore, if anyone is in Christ, the new creation has come: The old has gone, the new is here!"

Freedom / Triumph / New Life
(Flying with scars)

This stage is the reward, the unfolding of wings, the emergence into light. After all the pain, trauma, heartache, and torment... after the crawling, the hiding, the breaking and rebuilding... the butterfly takes flight, beautiful, free, and fully changed. This section is a celebration of becoming. The old is gone, and something new has taken its place. Not because everything is perfect, but because everything is different. These are the stories of healing, growth, and living in the fullness of lessons learned. Here, I share the moments when I felt light again, loved again, alive again. This is the better part of life, where purpose, peace, and freedom finally find their place.

Story 30: Top of the Ninth Inning

Nine was a good year. I was taken and placed into foster care with an amazing family. There were four other siblings there besides me: three girls and one boy. I had a hard time accepting the fact that my foster dad was there to protect me. All I had ever known men to be were mean and abusive. We would go on special trips, my siblings and I, to the park by the house. It was so refreshing and fun to know that we could just have fun being kids. During this time, I learned that going to church meant something special. We were in the children's choir, and I loved every minute of it!

Since I was the one who liked to cook, I got to help my foster mom cook most of the meals for the house. I had fun at school. It was a new feeling and experience to go to school every day; I wasn't used to that. I won the school spelling bee that year and got an award that I believe my foster mom still has. Our family didn't have a lot of extra money for us to go on trips, but what they always said was, "Being a family means more than all the money in the world". For some crazy reason, I didn't know that they may have said that to make us feel better for not going on trips, or because we didn't have much money. Either way, being a part of this family meant more than all the money in the world to me!

I learned how to crochet at that home. We each had to choose a special activity that we wanted to learn or do. I, unlike the other girls who were tomboys, picked crochet. My foster mom would sit with me for what seemed like hours, trying to teach me a single stitch. I would ask her, "Mrs. Julie, am I getting on your nerves?" She would often say with a giggle, "Sweetheart, my nerves left a long time ago. Anthony took them when we got married, but if I had any, you'll never get on them!" I would always say with a smile, "He has a lot of nerves, then!" We would just sit back and laugh. Well, it only took three months and about eight skeins of yarn, lol, and I had it! I was so excited! I even learned how to make a square. I made a scarf that year, even though it was not close to winter.

Every night when we went to bed, we would all hop in the "big bed", their bed, and read a scripture and pray. Oh, what joy filled us! Sometimes it's the little things that truly make a house into a home. Julie and Anthony, I believe, were angels sent to me to show me what a family is supposed to look like and be. Little did they know that in all of the pain, trauma, and abuse I experienced from my own family and foster families, the precious time I spent with them would be one of the few shining lights I could look back on. Indeed, it was the Top of the Ninth, but there were many more innings to go.

Personal Discovery:

In this story, I was finally happy and at peace. I did not know how long it was going to last, but what I did know was that I was going to enjoy it while it lasted. For so long, my life was shaped by trauma and abuse, by fear, by survival, by silence. I didn't know what peace felt like. Even in quiet moments, my body stayed tense, waiting for something to go wrong. I was always bracing for impact, carrying pain that never seemed to fully release.

But over time, through truth, through healing, through allowing myself to feel, I began to shift. Not all at once. There were still hard days, still triggers, still echoes of the past. But slowly, the storm inside me started to calm. I found safety in places I didn't expect: within myself, in people who listened without judgment, in the spaces I created where I could finally breathe. Now, I'm beginning to feel something I once thought was impossible: a newfound peace. The peace I had in this story was because everything was nearly perfect. The peace I've found today is not because everything is perfect, not because I've forgotten what I've been through, not because I have a new family, but because I've learned to reclaim my right to rest… to feel joy, to exist without fear defining me. Peace came when I stopped fighting myself and started honoring the strength it took to survive. I carry my past, but it no longer controls me. I've made it through. And in the quiet place where I used to fear and become tense, I've finally found myself whole, grounded, and free.

1. Can you remember a time when you felt deeply at peace? What contributed to that feeling?
2. When your life feels peaceful, how does it align with your values or priorities?
3. How do your spiritual or personal beliefs influence your view of peace?
4. What are small ways you can create peace, even in the middle of stress or uncertainty?

Story 31: A Chocolate Adventure

Surprise! We are going on a family vacation. I had never gone on a family vacation before, so this idea was new to me. But with this new beginning in life in a new city, with a new family, I was ready for the experience. I had only been in Huntsville for a few months. "Where are we going?" I thought. "Will I like it?" "We are going to Hershey, PA," Mom said. "Like the candy bar Hershey?" I asked. "Yep!" Mom said. It was going to be a while before we left for Hershey, so I had time to learn all that I could about this mysterious place. The time finally came. I thought the day was never going to come. We made our way to the airport and boarded the plane. I was excited because this was the first time since moving to Huntsville that I was flying, and this time, there was no intention of wanting to run.

We landed, and as soon as I got there, I swear it smelled like chocolate! Now it must have been just in my mind, because no one else smelled it. Lol! We checked into the resort, and we got settled in, and then we set up the plan for our upcoming day.

Our first stop was at the Hershey factory. Boy, I was excited! We were able to tour the factory and see how Hershey bars are created. We then were able to go to a movie. Now I thought this was going to be just a movie to explain how the Hershey company got started. However, I was in for a little surprise. This was a 4D show. I had only been to a regular movie before then, so this was a special treat for me. I had no idea what to expect from the movie, and then it started. I found out quickly what 4D meant. I had a blast! Things ran across my feet, which scared me at first; then it became fun. I smelled chocolate, and this time I was not the only one. Things were coming out of the screen, well, at least that is what the glasses made it look like.

Our next stop was a tour around the city, where I learned that Hershey has a house for kids to live in and go to school. These kids are much like me: they were without parents. Then it was off to eat dinner, and I went to Red Robin for the first time. It had an actual TV in the floor. Wow! Today, I'm still a Red Robin fan!

Sometimes it is the trivial things that matter most. A simple trip to Hershey, PA, for a chocolate adventure made me realize that people do take the time to enjoy life. This trip allowed me to let the little girl inside of me out. I had fun, and I honestly never thought that was possible. I now know I need to look beyond my past and realize that my future is far greater.

Personal Discovery:

In this story, I learned that fun isn't the opposite of pain; it's a powerful part of healing. After everything I have been through, I thought laughter was something I had to earn back. But joy doesn't wait for us to be "fixed." Sometimes it's what helps us start to feel whole again.

1. What does "having fun" mean to you personally?
2. Do you feel guilty when you allow yourself to have fun?

3. What fears come up when you allow yourself to relax or play?
4. When was the last time you truly had fun? What were you doing, and how did it feel?

Story 32: Winter Games

The weather was cold, and it was about to snow. I had been in Huntsville for two years, and my parents were away at the National Championship game that Alabama was playing in. I was staying at a friend's house while they were at the game, but the game was coming on and the family I was staying with didn't have the channel I needed to watch the game, so my parents told me to go home to watch the game. I came home early because it was going to snow, and I didn't want to be outside driving in the snow. My mom's dad lived with us, and he was at home when I got there. I walked in and was greeted with "What are you doing here?" I stood there and thought for a second. I mean, why does it matter? I live here too? However, all I said was "my mom told me to come home so I could watch the Bama game." He said, "Well, I'm in my room studying." I said, "OK," and walked back to my car. I was trying to figure out what to do. He did not say leave, but he was not welcoming me into my own home either. I just knew I needed to get out of the house at that moment. Not too long after I got back to the car, he came out and said I could come back into the house now. With much irritation, I got out of the car and went into the house.

While in the house, I took my bag to my room, and I went to my parents' room to use the bathroom. I usually used the bathroom in my parents' room just to avoid conflict with my mom's dad. He could be particular and set in his ways, and sharing a bathroom with him wasn't always the most inviting situation. I appreciate my parents for recognizing that and allowing me to use their bathroom. Now, in my parents' room, the toilet is separated from the rest of the bathroom. I turned on the light above the toilet while leaving the main light off. When I came out of the bathroom, he was waiting in the kitchen in the dark for me to come out. When I passed the kitchen, I was startled. He planned to prove that I was using the bathroom in the dark. Though it was none of his business if I was, the point was that I wasn't. He proceeded to yell at me for leaving the lights off as well as for leaving the back door unlocked, which I didn't do either.

We went around and around until I was in tears... angry tears. Mind you, I don't argue with folks. Remember, I'm the one who just goes silent and freezes because of all the trauma I've experienced. But this day... I clapped back. I was just so angry! Unfortunately, you can't talk to him and you can't reason with him... You just can't! After arguing with him until I was in tears, trying to tell him that I didn't do any of the things he accused me of, I called my mom, who was in California in the Rose Bowl, and it was right before kickoff. At the time, I didn't feel bad for calling her and interrupting her game experience; her dad needed to be dealt with, and I could no longer take it. She told me that she would get him to leave me alone, so I tried to calm down. To help calm myself down further, I called my Nana (see "Story 6: A Southern Grandmother"), who consoled me and then told me to apologize for yelling back at him. Apologizing to him ended up being a bad thing because a narcissist is always right, and there is no reasoning with one. So, of course, my apology started the argument back up. I finally just gave up and finished watching the game in my room with the door closed, hoping to never see him again... or at least not until my parents got back home. Frustrated and still in tears, I fell asleep and didn't finish the game. The argument didn't turn out the way I wanted, and I felt drained and defeated. But later, something unexpected happened. My mom told me how proud she was of me. I stood up for myself! I didn't realize how much of a breakthrough that was at the time, but looking back, it was a big deal. Oh yeah — although I missed it, we won, so... Roll Tide!

Personal Discovery:

I'm learning that avoiding conflict doesn't protect my peace; it only postpones my truth. I've spent so much time fearing what might happen if I speak up: the tension, the discomfort, the possibility of being misunderstood. But I'm slowly beginning to see that silence can cost just as much as confrontation, sometimes more. Trying to overcome the fear of conflict means I'm learning to sit with discomfort, to trust that I can handle hard conversations, and to believe that honesty doesn't have to come at the expense of connection. I'm not there yet, but each time I choose truth over avoidance, I feel a little braver, a little freer, and a little more myself.

1. What emotions come up for you during or after an argument?
2. What conflict in your life does this story of conflict remind you of?

3. What are you hoping to get out of a hard conversation: respect, validation, boundaries, or closeness?
4. Do you feel like your values or identity are being challenged during an argument?

Story 33: A Birthdays To Remember

There are things in life that we cannot change, like who we are born to or how we grow up. But one thing we can control is what our life will become. I had no idea, as a young toddler, how much suffering I would go through as a child and adolescent, but my adoptive parents made sure that, since they couldn't control who I was born to or how I was raised, they would influence what my life would become. Since my adoption, my birthdays have been opportunities for them to show me love, celebrate me, replace painful memories with happy ones, and help shape my future.

It was a hot day in mid-June, and once again, it was that time of year. Yep, my birthday... and this year marked my 25th birthday! Though it was one of my first birthdays in this new place and life, I didn't expect it to be anything special. I had only had one or two birthday parties before moving to Huntsville, and my birthday was never really celebrated. On my first birthday in Huntsville, my parents surprised me with a keyboard! I was shocked and excited to get something I had wanted for years and couldn't afford. At the same time, feelings of "I don't deserve this" tried to creep in and ruin it for me. Still, this set a new precedent for how I would experience birthdays: receiving gifts, being celebrated, being loved. I was thankful, but I sure didn't expect what was about to happen this year!

My parents had been gone all day. I just assumed they were really, really busy and, as usual, I was thinking, "Oh my goodness, they are never coming back... like this is finally the time that they are really leaving me, and they chose my birthday to do it." I know, I know! It's funny where your mind goes when you have been through some things! I decided that I would get ready, pack a few things, and leave before they came back… you know, from leaving me and all. (I'm telling you… that feeling of abandonment is a hard one to overcome, even when your new family gives you no reason to think they'll leave you!) About midday, my friend called me and told me to get ready because she was coming to pick me up to take me to a friend's party. I did not want to go at all, but what else was I doing? Nothing but trying to figure out how and when to leave my parents before they left me. So, reluctantly, I got ready and waited for her to pick me up.

She picked me up and we didn't go far. We pulled up to this clubhouse at the apartments down the street from the house. I was irritated because I, for one, didn't want to go to this party, and, secondly, the whole fear-of-my-parents-leaving-me situation was at the forefront of my mind. However, I tried my best not to have an attitude about it. I put on a smile and got out of the car. Then, it happened! There, across the parking lot and near the door of the clubhouse, was a piñata hanging from the tree… and it was SPONGEBOB!! Like really! "Who lives in a pineapple under the sea?" SpongeBob! So now, I don't care what the party was about, I wanted to stay outside and play with the SpongeBob piñata. "Okay, okay, Shay," I scorned myself, "You're 25 now. Let's act your age and go in." I put my attitude back on like I was putting on a new shirt and walked toward the door.

As I walked into the clubhouse, I heard a resounding, "Surprise!" My first reaction was to want to run and hide. What in the world was going on, and who were all these people?? As soon as the shock from the surprise wore off, I realized that I knew all the people there, and then that warm love from those people overtook me. My next thought was, "Oh, wow! Well, this is nice, and since the party was for me, can I go back outside and play with the SpongeBob piñata?" But my mom grabbed my hand and took me around the rooms of the clubhouse, and, wow! This was not just a birthday party; this was a walk through my childhood, but in a good way. There was a station that represented every milestone birthday that the "normal" child might celebrate, each decorated with age-appropriate decorations and activities.

It started at age 1 with a real smash cake and all. I thought, "Surely, they are not wanting me to really eat this cake with my fingers!" Oh yes! They did. Me... not-at-all, somewhat, okay, REALLY having OCD, twitched on the inside a bit as I, like a 1-year-old, sat on the floor and ate cake with my hands. My mom knew to have cleaning supplies for me once I got up because she knew my not-at-all, but really a lot of OCD tendencies (okay, I'll admit it, I may slightly be in denial). She knew I was going to need assistance immediately!

The next station was age 5, and we played "Pin the Hat on the Picture of the Birthday Girl." There was an (uncomfortably) huge picture of me on the wall, and we all had to pin a hat on me on the picture while blindfolded. 5-year-old fun! Next was age 9, and finally the SpongeBob piñata! Several of us swung at it, and I was able to swing until all the candy came out! I hated to hurt SpongeBob, but I appreciated him so much for dropping my favorite candies!

We had a balloon step contest for age 13, where everyone tried to step on and pop everyone else's balloons, and then a Sweet 16 dance with my daddy for age 16. This was the best part of the day, yes, even above my time with SpongeBob. I had never danced with any man before, and my dad made sure that this dance was special… as if I were turning 16. "Dance with My Father" by Luther Vandross was playing in the background, and I was given a sash and a tiara. A gentle hand was stretched out for me to take. I felt like the princess that I should have been all of my life. Boy, was this moment special! To celebrate age 21, there was a toast to the Birthday Girl with sparkling juice and all! We were doing it up at that point. Several of the attendees said kind words about me that, if I'm honest, took me close to 10 years to believe. By the time we got to celebrating 25, my then-current birthday year, I didn't think anything could get any better! I opened gifts, and there was a trivia game about the year I was born.

I was just so overwhelmed with love and gratitude. The food was made up of all of my favorites. It was a day filled with celebrating me just for being me. My heart was so full that day; the opportunity to celebrate all those milestones will forever be etched in my mind. My parents made sure that all those years lost while growing up were regained with more fun, love, and excitement than I could ever have expected. It was truly a *birthdays* to remember! People left the party saying that this was one of the best birthday parties they had ever attended, yet I don't think they could have enjoyed it more than me!

Personal Discovery:

At my 25th birthday, I learned that I could replace bad memories with positive ones or change bad experiences into good ones. To be honest, I never thought that could be the case, but I was given a second chance. Getting a second chance feels like grace in motion, an invitation to write a new chapter.

1. What is your personal second-chance experience, or what can you do for yourself to create a second-chance experience?
2. Is there anything holding you back from allowing yourself to enjoy your second chance experience(s)?
3. What does getting a second chance do for your healing?
4. Is there any part of you that feels like you don't deserve this second chance? Where does that belief come from?

Kar'Michay Pope

Story 34: Sweet Home Alabama

It is fall in the Deep South! You know what that means, right? Yep! Are you ready for some football?! Like everyone, when I first moved to Alabama, I was given a choice… well, actually, in my case, it was chosen for me. My new mom was a graduate of the University of Alabama and a die-hard fan. So, obviously, I was choosing Alabama. However, I had no idea what the point of football was. They just seemed to be trying to get the ball, hitting each other so that the other would let go of the ball. Then you get points for running down the field while being chased. Just crazy, in my opinion! There was no point for me to even care about this evil sport.

In this family, watching football on Saturday and going to church on Sunday were things we rarely missed. So, since I couldn't watch anything else on TV, I watched football. Over time, my dad began to explain what was going on, that it wasn't just a bunch of men trying to get the ball… there's actually more to it. And, for the record, my dad taught me because he's the patient one between him and my mom when it comes to football. She seems to have some form of religion that keeps her from explaining football while she's watching "her game", and she sure does seem to have a lot of games. Thank God for my dad!! So, the more we watched, the more I began to understand it. Then, for some strange reason, I started to like it! This crazy sport… I actually like this crazy sport! I can't believe it.

Oh, it turns out that being an Alabama fan has its perks. There is a secret society-type language called "Roll Tide". You can be walking down the street, see someone with Alabama paraphernalia on, and immediately y'all say Roll Tide to each other. It's amazing, and I love it. And it doesn't just happen in Alabama. You can be in Florida, New York, California, at a wedding, at a funeral, at church. It doesn't matter. The Roll Tide secret society will always embrace you! When I first moved to Alabama, my mom went to the games all the time by herself. Eventually, my dad started going too. I would stay home and watch while they attended, yelling and screaming and, of course, saying Roll Tide! But the day I found out I was going to an actual Alabama game, I think I almost passed out.

It was Christmas yet again, and my parents saved the best gift for last; however, to me, every gift was the best gift. I never wanted much and never asked for much. I mean, just to have gifts that weren't taken away from me was amazing! I opened a box and there they were: tickets to an Alabama game! "Like, no way! Are they serious?! Are they really serious about this? I'M going to an Alabama game?? This must be a joke or a dream." All of those thoughts were going through my head. However, it wasn't either one. I had never been to a game in person. I couldn't wait until all the seasons, winter, spring, and summer, had passed because after that comes fall, and that's football season.

It was a long wait, but football season finally came, and when it was time to go to my first game, I was fully decked out in my Alabama gear. We were on our way to Tuscaloosa, home of the Alabama Crimson Tide. We got there and parked. We then took a shuttle to the stadium. I was so nervous! I had no idea what to expect. Walking outside the stadium was a bit overwhelming. There were thousands of people! I mean, so many people! Then I walked into the stadium and all the energy! I can't even begin to tell you how many people were there. It was just a huge sea of crimson and white colored shirts. All chanting, "Sweet Home Alabama, Roll Tide Roll". I made my way to my seat just as the national anthem started.

As soon as the national anthem was finished, it was time for the teams to come out onto the field. The visiting team ran out first, and then the Alabama team ran onto the field. The rush, the adrenaline, all the emotions came out of me as I was yelling and singing, "Yay Alabama", Alabama's fight song. "Yay Alabama" stopped, and it was time to get the game started. It was Alabama's ball. I was so excited because I finally understood why they were running with the ball. He's at the 30, the 20, the 10, 5, touchdown Alabama! I couldn't believe it; I was watching it IN PERSON! I was hugging and high-fiving people I didn't know, and I was loving every moment of it.

Just when I thought it couldn't get any better, the Million Dollar Band came on the field playing during halftime, and I was, at that moment, back in high school playing in the marching band with my flute up and down the field. It was simply amazing. Every aspect of the game brought me joy, and we came away with a Bama win! Now I have season tickets, and it's just normal for me to go to a game. I want to always remember the experience of that first game so that I can realize what a huge blessing it is for me to attend so many games now. Who would've thought that this abused and forgotten girl who didn't understand a thing about football would enjoy having season tickets and going to some of the biggest games in college football? I'm blessed and I'm thankful. And until the next time, Roll Tide!

Personal Discovery:

I discovered that joy has a way of showing up in the moments I once only hoped for. Going to the football game wasn't just fun, it was a reminder that dreams don't have to be big to be meaningful. That moment, surrounded by energy, laughter, and life, felt like a celebration of how far I've come. It was more than a game; it was a promise fulfilled, a glimpse of happiness after hard days, and proof that hope was never wasted.

1. Is there something that you thought you would never like that you now enjoy?
2. What happened that gave you the opportunity to embrace and relish it?
3. What's something that you need to allow yourself to try?
4. Do you ever feel guilty for enjoying yourself? Where does that come from?

Kar'Michay Pope

Story 35: Trapped

(Content Warning: This story contains descriptions of sexual abuse and/or violence. Please take care of yourself while reading.)

Staring out the window, the sun is shining and the birds are chirping, but I'm scared I'll never experience it because I'm trapped. Inside my head, it's not sunny, it's pouring, and the only things that are chirping are the thoughts in my head that are screaming to get out. But they too are trapped in cages surrounded by fences that are surrounded by barbed wire fences and bound by chains. Where and when did this entrapment begin? Perhaps it was the first time I was touched or the moment my innocence was taken. Maybe it was lost in the I love you's that I never received, or from every touch, slap, kick, or snatched by the hair experience I received. I'm on a merry-go-round wanting so desperately to get off, but I can't move. The force that's pinning me down is greater than the strength I have left to give.

Mom says pray, Dad says pray, and while yes, prayer is good, who's gonna silence the screams of the broken little girl inside of me enough to think of the words to pray? How many prayers until this pain goes away? I used to think that everyone hurt like me — that every girl was being beaten and raped inside their homes. But then I realized this was not true, and I want to be angry… but anger is trapped with fear, and once again I'm alone. I was about 30 when it happened yet again. This time, however, I put myself in an unsafe situation. He was about 6'4, 300 pounds of pure muscle. I had met him at his job. He seemed pretty cool, so when he asked me to hang out, I thought, "Yeah, sure, OK." I had not had a man pay that much attention to me in a long time, so I was a little interested. Even though I didn't want him to touch me, I didn't mind him trying to be my friend. We had been talking on the phone for a few weeks, so when he asked me to stop by, it seemed and felt okay.

The first time I went there, he was a perfect gentleman. We sat and talked, got to know each other more, and then I left. Therefore, it didn't feel like a big deal for me to stop by his house once I left a friend's birthday dinner a few weeks later. Things were okay for the first 30 minutes, then things went south. He pinned me to the couch with his arm against my throat. I froze. I didn't know what to do or how to feel. He broke the button off my favorite jeans, trying to get my pants down. Finally, he moved his arm from my throat and used both hands to get my pants off. My jeans are now half off, and my purple pennies are ripped half off. Then it happens, he inserts himself inside me. This seemed to hurt far worse than the uncle. The size and force of his penis made me feel as if it were touching my uterus. It hurt, and with every stroke, I could feel more and more pain. It made me bleed. When he finished, he kissed me and got up to let me go. I lay there for a moment, unable to move.

Once again, I was trapped; my mind was somewhat alive, but my body felt dead. I left, got in my car, drove home, and sat in the garage. My parents were out of town, so I was alone... alone yet again. I was alone long enough for my mind to be lost in emotions, emotions, and feelings that seemed once again locked in a cage with barbed wire fences. Maybe I wear rape on me like a badge of honor, and when men see me, it's like giving them an open invitation to my body. I feel like the more I tried to fight it, the more my body seemed to invite it. My body had gotten accustomed to the abuse; it didn't know how it felt to be free. "Maybe this is why it keeps happening. My body is no longer a temple; it is no longer mine, it is just a garden variety for men to choose from. I can no longer be found by joy, and I have just succumbed to death. I am trapped and there's no one left to save me."

Personal Discovery:

After moving to Huntsville and being free from the trauma that I grew up with, I experienced trauma again. After finding safety, only to find more trauma, I didn't feel like myself anymore. I felt like a stranger living inside a body that had learned how to hide. I smiled when I was supposed to. I functioned. But inside, I felt stuck, like I was screaming behind a wall no one else could see. The pain wasn't always visible, but it was constant. I didn't know how to be free, because safety had once meant shutting down, staying small, staying silent. I wasn't just trapped in the past; I was trapped in the ways I learned to survive my past. Numbness became normal. Dissociation felt like protection. I didn't know how to reach myself, let alone trust anyone else to find me. But somewhere along the way, I began to notice the small cracks in places where light began to filter through. A moment of honesty. A deep breath. A feeling I didn't push away. I started realizing that healing isn't about going back to who I was before; I'll never be that person again. It's about meeting who I am now, with compassion, and slowly helping that part of me feel safe enough to step forward.

I'm learning that I'm not broken, I'm layered. And even if I still feel trapped some days, I now know there's a way out. And that the real me, the one who survived, is still in there, waiting to be fully seen and set free... again.

1. Have you ever felt "trapped?" What does it feel like inside when you feel that way?
2. How do you carry pain from your past with you... mentally, physically, and emotionally?
3. What would it look like to feel "free"? Not necessarily "healed," but less trapped by the pain of your past? Identify the differences in your own experience of being free vs. being healed.
4. If your pain could speak, what would it say? If your strength could speak, what would it say in response? Write a dialogue between the two.

Kar'Michay Pope

Story 36: I Got Soul

It was a beautiful Saturday morning. My Nana had just flown in the night before, and I was so excited about that. Even though it was a special day for me, I just could not believe that she was in town! The big day was finally here; it was my graduation day! When I moved to Alabama, I wondered if I would be able to even attend college. I began by working in third and fourth-grade workbooks to gain the knowledge I missed in my jagged and unstable upbringing. Yep! You read it right! I was a young adult, in my twenties, with a high school diploma, learning what I should have learned in late elementary school and beyond. With my mom's help, I worked my way through these workbooks and gradually made my way to high school workbooks. Then, I applied to a local community college and began taking classes. I remember thinking I would fail each and every class. I just didn't think I could possibly be good enough to pass college classes. Three years later, I received my two-year degree! Wow! I did it! But I didn't stop there. I went on to work on my bachelor's degree, and again, I thought it wasn't possible. But here we were, on this day, with the impossible about to happen! I was going to walk across the stage to accept my bachelor's degree.

I woke up ready to go… early enough to do my makeup and hair. My dress was a navy-blue skater dress, which matched almost perfectly with my school colors. I skipped breakfast that morning. I think I was too nervous to eat anything. On this day, not only was I graduating, but

I was also singing the National Anthem and the Alma Mater at the ceremony. What an honor this was! The best part of me having to make the nearly hour-long drive to my graduation was the fact that my Nana was riding with me. Everything is wonderful when Nana is around! We arrived at the school, and she helped me get myself together and ready to join the graduates in the waiting area. She then left to go take her seat and save seats for the rest of the family. Although I was able to march with my class, because I was on program to sing, my seat was right next to the stage. The speaker got up and greeted everyone, a prayer was given, then it was my turn to sing. Although I had sung the national anthem at a few other events here and there, including the graduating class of the previous semester, this was MY graduation... for my bachelor's degree! Oh my goodness, I was so nervous, but not nearly as nervous as I was excited to walk across that stage. I sang, and I think I hid my nerves pretty well. Then I took my seat. The graduation proceeded as normal, and soon it was my turn to walk the stage. The speaker called my name, and there was then an eruption of excitement from my family. You really can't imagine what it feels like to have family support when you grew up with your natural family not only not supporting you, but rejecting you. The ceremony finished, and it was time for me to lead my fellow graduates and the attendees in singing the school's Alma Mater. I got chocked up while singing it, because not only was this a special moment for me, but it was also the closing of yet another chapter of what I was beginning to realize is an amazing book... my life (who would've "thunk" it!).

Kar'Michay Pope

When graduation was over, it was time for the family to go out to eat. I was extra hungry after skipping breakfast, and it was cool because all my family that was there were going out to eat with me. I was also extra excited because we had planned a huge 80's 80s-themed graduation party for that night. After taking lots and lots of pictures in my cap and gown, including a picture with the President of the school (whom I knew personally, because I served as the president of the SGA my last year there... yeah... ME... president of the SGA!), it was finally time to leave. So, I started walking to my car, talking with my family, laughing, and enjoying the moment. We were all walking out to the cars together, and I didn't pay attention to the fact that everyone was walking with me to MY car. One of my aunties asked if I could give her a ride to the restaurant, and of course, I said yes. I realize now that this was just a ploy to get me to look in her direction. I was so caught up in the high of the morning that her plan failed, and I didn't notice anything around her.

Soon after that, my dad called my name and told me to look his way so he could snap another picture. It took me a second to find him because he had walked to the row of parking spaces across from my car. When I did find him, all I saw was a beautiful, off-white Kia Soul with a huge bow on the windshield and a sign that read "Congratulations Kar'Michay"! I could not believe it! A new car (well, new to me)?! Not only that, it was my dream car! My dream car was sitting right in front of me! My mom always said that while some people have a dream car of a Mercedes or a BMW or Tesla, my dream car was... a Kia Soul. In utter excitement, I jumped and screamed and jumped and screamed and yelled and screamed and ran to my dad, who was standing right next to the driver's door. I was jumping and running so hard that my graduation gown, hat, and stole came off and were lying on the ground. (My family joked that I was dancing out of my clothes like David in the Bible.) When I made it to my dad, with nothing but my graduation cords still around me (and my navy dress, of course), I jumped and screamed and danced and shook my hands and screamed some more. Then I stopped in mid-jump and asked, "Wait! Is this a rental?!" My dad laughed and said, "We wouldn't do you like that!" I really could not believe that my DREAM car was there, right in front of me. I could TOUCH it! It was mine, and all I kept saying was "Oh my gosh, oh my gosh, my car, it's my car!" I turned to my mom and pounced on, I mean... hugged, her. It was one of those long, take-it-in, I-can't-thank-you-enough hugs, and I cried. Then I hugged my dad and cried some more. Then, what just happened hit me again, and I started screaming and jumping all over again! Mind you, I hadn't even touched the car yet.

My dad said, amid my screaming, "Open the door." I reached to grab the handle, and he said, "All you have to do is press the button." Of course, I got excited and started screaming and jumping again. When I opened the door, I found that it had peanut butter leather seats. They were gorgeous! I just stood there, staring in awe. My family had to tell me to sit in the car, so I did. They then told me to look up and, you guessed it, I started screaming again, "Oh my gosh, there is a sunroof!" My dad handed me the key, I started the car, and he told me to put the car in reverse.

When I did, I yelled again and said, "Oh my gosh! There is a backup camera!" I mean, this car had everything that I ever wanted in a car. It was truly my dream car. Years later, I look at it and say that I cannot believe it is mine. It is beautiful in all its ways. Once again, what I thought would never happen to me did: on one day, two of my dreams became a reality. I got a bachelor's degree, and I got Soul, and it felt (and still feels) so good!

Personal Discovery:

With my unstable upbringing, I was delayed in my education, but I eventually learned that a delay doesn't mean an impossibility. With hard work and dedication, I was able to achieve my dreams, but I will admit, I questioned if I could.

1. What dreams do you have that you've given up on or question if you can achieve?
2. What small steps can you take to move towards accomplishing your dream? Remember, dreams really can come true!
3. After achieving my goal, I was celebrated by my parents. Who in your life is celebrating you?
4. How can you show them appreciation for the support they've given you?

Story 37: Over the Ledge

It was a bright, sunny, beautiful day in Nashville, not a cloud in the Sky. I woke up with plans to go to my outpatient, half-day session and come back to the house. I was in pain that morning. I had been in pain for a few days. Not physical pain, emotional pain. My outpatient sessions had stirred up so much pain, and that pain was just sitting in my heart, mind, and body. It was overwhelming; nevertheless, I got dressed and left the house. I pulled into the parking lot of the outpatient facility, and then it hit me... what was I doing all of this for? Things just seem to go back to the same way they were and had always been, so what's the difference now? I'd come to the conclusion that I was tired of living on this roller coaster of life: peace and pain. It was just a vicious cycle that I thought would never end. Every time I think I finally have a bit of peace, it is not long before there is more pain, and sometimes the pain is worse than the peace seemed to fix. I said, "Enough of it all!" In the past, I had tried almost everything to end my life, and nothing worked. I needed a surefire way for this to work this time.

So, I pulled out my phone and searched the internet for bridges in Nashville, and wow! I found one, and it wasn't far from me. I drove there in tears. I was just over all of the pain. I was just over feeling alone. I wanted all of the noise inside my head to stop, and I was actually at peace that I had finally found something to make it stop. After about a 15-minute ride, I pulled up to the bridge and paused for a second. I thought about what I would be leaving behind, so I wrote a letter to the ones I love in hopes that they would just understand. I just knew in my heart they would. I mean, they love me, right? They don't want me to be in so much pain. Who would want that?

I walked up to the bridge and stood there. I looked out and silently said a prayer. I prayed for my family. My prayer was "Dear Lord, please protect my family from any pain they may have. Give them peace and comfort them and wrap them in your arms. Allow them to understand that I am finally at peace; let them know that it's ok. Let them not be hurt or think it was their fault. Give them joy instead of sadness." I also prayed for myself saying, "Dear Lord, please forgive me for what I am about to do. This pain is too great and it's more than I can bear. I tried all that I could, and you know that nothing has changed. So please forgive me for giving up. I'm sorry if I'm letting you down. I just can't take it anymore. God, you see my shattered and broken heart and you know this pain I feel. I have asked you to take it away, yet you seem to give me more. All that I have been through is simply too much. God, please love me despite what I'm about to do. I love you more than life itself." I felt good after this prayer, knowing I was honest with God and really shared my heart.

I took a moment to look upon the horizon and bask in its beauty, not realizing that this was exactly what I needed to do inside. I needed to look at and beyond the horizon of my right-now agony. I counted the cars that passed under the bridge and hoped that they also would not be impacted by my decision. I took the time to listen to the birds and feel the wind as it grazed my face. I noticed the grass and how green it was and the fullness of the leaves on the trees. At that moment, I was at complete peace. I felt that I was finally doing what was best for me. I put one hand on the bridge rail, and then one leg over the ledge. I envisioned the feeling of flying. I closed my eyes and just as I was about to let go a man

on a motorcycle pulled up and started walking towards me. I tried to ignore him.

As he walked towards me, I already knew what I was going to say to get rid of him. I did not want to be talked out of it. I did not want to explain my reasoning. I just came to the bridge for a purpose, and I wanted to complete that purpose. However, he had kind eyes as he approached me and didn't ask me what I was doing. He just asked if I was thinking of doing something. That caught me off guard. I was ready for a fight, and he was not there to give me one. As I was standing there, I found myself unable to lie, unable to tell him all the things I had planned to tell him. I began telling this stranger my hurt and sharing with him my pain. He, like a friend, gently walked me down the walkway off the bridge.

He talked to me and truly just wanted to listen; he wanted to help. I found out that he was an off-duty officer and, even though he was so nice, that scared me a bit. I asked him if he was going to take me to jail. He said, "Of course not, I just want to be here for you." The crazy part about that whole encounter is... I believed him! I felt comfortable with him. Soon, other officers came and talked to me. A social worker came over to talk to me as well. For a second, I thought, "Please just leave me alone. I already know what I want to do. I have everything planned out.

Stop talking to me! Let me feel the way I'm feeling, and let me do what I came to do!" Then I thought, "God, why did you send all these people here? You won't even let me die... AGAIN." I was angry at God. I didn't understand why he wanted me to stay in this pain. Why did he want me to suffer? What was it all for? The social worker that just happened to be there was kind of a coincidence because she was working in the field I was in school for and wanted to go into after I graduated. After a while, an ambulance came and took me to the hospital. I hated this part of the day because I knew what this meant. I was going to inpatient again. I was able to go back to the inpatient place I was in before, so at least I was going somewhere familiar.

Eventually, I was safe enough to be released from inpatient. It took a while because my pain was so great, and I just struggled to accept that I was supposed to continue to live with it. As you can imagine, even after years of counseling, there was so much pain and trauma that I had to work through, and trust me, the pain of working through trauma is almost as bad as the pain of enduring the trauma! I'm not going to lie, sometimes I do wish that I was able to jump off that bridge. Emotional pain, which can be the worst kind, is still a part of my life some days, and sometimes I wonder if it is worth it to fight through that pain in order to see and realize my potential and purpose.

Looking back now, I see all that I've accomplished, all of the lives that I would not have touched, and all the things I wouldn't have done if I had jumped. I realize that I went through that for a reason. I can use my experience to help someone else who may want to go over the ledge themselves. If that's you, let me tell you... You have to try to look beyond your feelings. You must look beyond the horizon, beyond what you can see and feel. Try to believe that there is something beyond what you're currently experiencing because there is! You don't know what that is yet because you haven't tapped into it, but you have to trust and believe that greater is there waiting for you to attain it. I didn't believe it was there, and sometimes even today I question it. I've learned to constantly tell myself that there is something beyond my current feelings. My goal and passion must be figuring out what that is, what's beyond what I feel, and going after it instead of just honing in on what my feelings are right now. Instead of giving all of my energy to my current feelings, I've decided that from now on I will only give my energy to things that add to my growth!

Several weeks later, after lots of internal work in both inpatient and outpatient facilities, my family and I were able to meet up with the officer who had met me on the bridge as I was about to go over the ledge. We had dinner with him and his wife. We were so grateful and happy to meet again, and my parents were grateful and happy to meet the man who saved their daughter's life. Officer Jordan was in the right place at the right time and said the right things that kept me from doing what I thought at the time was the right thing to do. And here I was thinking that God was punishing me! For a precious few moments in time, Officer Jordan and I were connected with a bond that I hope to never be broken. He and his beautiful wife will forever have a special place in my heart.

Personal Discovery:

I discovered that at my breaking point, I wasn't losing everything; I was shedding what I was never meant to carry. It felt like the end, but it was actually the beginning of something deeper: a raw, honest surrender. In that space where I had nothing left to give, I found the quiet presence of God still holding me together. My breaking point didn't destroy me; it broke the illusion that I had to be strong on my own. And in that breaking, something beautiful began to rebuild.

1. What did your breaking point look and feel like?
2. What emotions came up when you were at your breaking point?
3. What helped you survive or move through that point?
4. Looking back, is there anything that "broke" that needed to?

Story 38: The Hills that Roll

Being in inpatient is hard; however, sometimes I believe that being in outpatient is harder. Outpatient makes you truly focus on yourself and all your mental junk. Like most there, I got the royal escort from one building (inpatient facility) to the next. They were so gracious to take the time to give me a personal escort! In other words, they wanted to make sure I didn't run. I'm not gonna lie and say I didn't think about it a time or two, but hey, they were holding onto my most prized possessions: my shoelaces! As I walked through the door, I just wondered if this was really happening. I heard the door close behind me, and I knew for sure that this was all too real. Right before I walked into the room, I felt instant fear. Were they going to judge me for coming back? What was our fearless leader going to say? Was she going to give me the look of disapproval? I had no idea what was waiting for me behind the big brown door. With much hesitation, I went in, and to my surprise, I was instantly welcomed. Although, truth be told, I think I was more excited to see my chair in all its glory waiting for me to grace its presence with my butt.

When I sat down, I felt very anxious. There were a few new faces... a few that were familiar, but mostly new faces. I was unsure how they were going to receive me. Would they judge me? Would they look at me with shame in their eyes because of my history? Would they even accept me? These were all the questions I had roaming around my head. However, as time went on, I realized that

Kar'Michay Pope

even though we didn't share the same story completely, we were all on the same journey and road to healing.

There were a few that made a strong impact on me. There was Kendra, with the long blonde hair and the contagious laugh, who never seemed to not be without an encouraging word to others, but I'm not sure if she thought of herself as worthy enough to have them spoken to her. There was Jasmine, with the most beautiful smile, who never seemed to realize she was good enough all by herself... that her grace and poise made her who she was and not all the things she was searching after. There was Jennifer, who brought me beautiful flowers, whom I really wanted to grab and say, "Spoil yourself the way you nurture and spoil everyone else! You are worth more. Just give yourself a fair chance." Tenisha, who was my coloring partner, was beautiful inside and out. She just needed to be told, "You're worth it. You are worth life," and believe it. I can't leave out Britney, who was always late coming back from smoke breaks. She shared my foster care journey. I wanted to just hug her and tell her that she was always good enough, worthy enough, and wanted. Then there was Salem, who didn't seem to realize she was stronger than she gave herself credit for. Let's not forget that favorite aunt of the group, Sharon. She is loving, caring, and feisty. She's not afraid to tell it like it is, and you never had to wonder if she cared because she'd always show it. Finally, the leader of this wild pack: Rachael. She will encourage and kick you in the butt all at the same time with one look. She's always in a pretzel position, and she's one whose impact on my life I will never forget!

I may not have been exactly where I thought I should be as I walked out the big brown door of The Hills that Roll for the last time, but I know for sure I wasn't where I was when I walked through it. It's a bittersweet moment to be leaving a home away from home. Thoughts run through your head, "I wonder what this new life will look like." "Will I make it?" "Will I end up right back here?" One thing's for sure, whichever way I go, I know that just because I'm wandering doesn't mean that I'm lost.

Personal Discovery:

In this story, I went from being completely afraid of what was lying ahead of me to being walked through a process towards healing. In the end, I felt loved and supported. There were moments in my healing journey when fear wrapped around me so tightly, I didn't know how to breathe through it. I feared remembering too much, of feeling too deeply, of breaking apart in a way I couldn't put back together. I didn't trust safety, not because it wasn't there, but because I didn't recognize it. I had lived too long in survival mode to believe I could rest.

But somewhere in the middle of all that fear, someone stayed. It was a person, it was a quiet presence, a therapist, a friend, and even just a part of me I hadn't met yet. I was still scared, but I wasn't alone anymore. And that changed everything. Support didn't take the fear away, but it gave me something solid to hold onto while I walked through it. What I've discovered is that courage doesn't mean I'm never afraid; it means I keep going even when I am, because now I know I don't have to do it alone. The fear may rise, but so does the support. And that's where healing begins, in the space between what terrifies me and who's holding me through it.

1. Has fear ever crippled you? Name a time when fear tried to keep you from something that was good and helpful for you.
2. What lessons have you learned on your healing journey? Try to come up with at least 10. Write them and remind yourself of them regularly.
3. Describe what "healed" means to you. Is it a destination or a process?
4. How are you showing yourself grace while on this healing journey?

Story 39: Never Forgotten

Happy Birthday to you, happy birthday to you, happy birthday Jeremiah, Happy birthday to you. On December 6, 2008, a small #1 candle sits on a small cake. The flame flickers as wind from our hands makes the light dance across the candle. It's just the three of us, but that is all I need; the people that matter the most are here. "Happy Birthday to my g-baby," Mom says. "Thank you for being the light in a very dark time and a blessing amid despair. You have made our lives better just by being born. Your g-momma loves you, and I'll always be grateful for your life," Mom shared. Dad was up next, and he said, "Jeremiah, I second everything that your g-momma said," with a small smile and chuckle. "You were right on time, your life mattered, and what you did for your mother changed her life for the better. I love you very much."

Now it was my turn. What do I say? What words can I speak that will soothe my broken heart? I am to say words that should fall on little ears that I can hold and touch. Instead, I am speaking to heaven's gate because the hard fact was that Jeremiah, my baby, was gone, and he's never coming back.

However, this was his day, and it was a day to celebrate the love he brought to my heart when I needed it most. "So, happy first birthday, Miah man. I can't believe that you are one already. Time has flown by. You are so special to me, and, just like your g-momma and g-dad said, you were born for a purpose, and your life brought about so many beautiful blessings. I thank God for you and for allowing me to be your mother. I hope that I am making you proud" are the words that gently flowed from my lips.

Visions of Jeremiah smashing cake with his hands, me having a full panic attack because he is a mess, Mom stopping me from cleaning him up, and Daddy taking a million videos and pictures of the whole event flash in my head. They bring a smile to my face and a frown to my heart, knowing that I will never get this — I'll never have these memories. Although, I don't or won't have these memories of sitting around a table every year with the most important people, celebrating one of the most important persons in my life, every year I do get to remember giving birth to the most amazing son ever and I do get to celebrate his beautiful, short-lived life with my family every year for his birthday.

Sometimes I forget to take a moment and just bask in the fact that God knew just what I needed at the time, and he gave it to me. Oftentimes, we can get so caught up in mourning the death that we forget to celebrate the life, which is equally, if not more important. I cannot do anything to bring Jeremiah back, but what I can do is make sure that he is never forgotten.

Personal Discovery:

In this story, I was fighting my way back to being okay with not being okay. My son was gone, and a piece of me felt empty. Losing my child shattered everything I believed about the world, about life, about myself. There are no words big enough for the hole that kind of loss leaves behind. It's not just pain, it's a silence that screams, a future that never gets to unfold. I felt lost, broken, and completely undone when Jeremiah passed. People told me time would heal, but time only made the absence more real. I carried guilt, anger, and questions no one could answer. I wondered how I was supposed to keep living when part of me was gone.

But slowly, in the stillness of the ache, I began to understand that grief is love with nowhere to go. And though the pain didn't disappear, something else began to grow beside it, resilience, memory, meaning. "Enough is enough" wasn't about the pain ending; it was about refusing to let that pain erase the love, the joy, and the connection that still exists. I live now with the ache and the love side by side. My children may not be here physically, but their presence lives on in who I am becoming. I am forever changed, not just by the loss, but by the love that came before it.

1. How has your grief changed over time?
2. How did the person you lost influence the person you are today?
3. What do you miss most about your loved one?
4. What does "Never forgetting them" mean to you?

Kar'Michay Pope

Story 40: From Trauma to Triumph

Never did I ever think that this chapter in my life would manifest, that there would be days that I would wake up happy to see daylight. Now I am not going to say that every day is a great day, but what I can say is that every day is a blessed one, full of opportunities to make it a great day. Growing up, things were hard, actually "hard" does not even come close to describing what my life was like growing up. There were more days than not that I hated to see another day. I would often tell God that He did not love me and wanted to punish me, and that is why He woke me up every day. I grew up in an atmosphere of chaos, destruction, denigration, abandonment, hatred, violence, neglect, and depravity. Peace seemed so far from reality, and happiness seemed to always evade me. I hear childhood memories are some of the best memories… days in which you have no worries or cares, and you are free to just live your life. Well, not in my case. My memories are filled with heartache and pain, so much heartache and pain. From one rape to another, from one beating to the next beating, foster home to foster home. The only consistent thing in my life was abuse. In some form or fashion, abuse was coming. How bad it was going to get, I never could have imagined. How I lived through it, I'll never know. Every now and then, I got glimpses of what my life should and could be like through the eyes of others. Seeing other kids happy provided a little hope that I, too, could one day have what they had. As much as my hope wanted to grab ahold of these dreams, my despair wanted to embrace my realities.

Then I met a lady... a lady who became my sissy and then my mommy... and things in my life started to change. She saw me for me. She saw what I so desperately tried to hide behind a mask (actually, several masks). She dared to go where others have not even tried to go. I tried hard to keep her away... to only let her get as close as I wanted her to get, as close as I had allowed others to have gotten, which was actually not close at all. I did not want her behind my mask. I was too ashamed of what was behind the mask. I didn't love myself, and I didn't believe she or anyone could either. However, she would not leave. She just kept fighting me for me, no matter how many times I fought her, trying to convince her NOT to fight for me. I didn't believe I was worth fighting for. I was running, and the truth was, deep down inside, I think I wanted to be caught, but only by the right one... one who would help me find that joyful place that I found glimpses of as a child. Nevertheless, I was determined that my history would not repeat itself. You see, every time someone got close or I got close to someone, they ended up hurting me and then leaving me. My days seemed to run together, and it felt, sometimes, as if time stood still. My life was passing me by, and I did not know how to stop it. This time, I was not going to let this continue to happen with yet another so-called "mom" or "aunt" or "friend". I was not going to allow ANOTHER person to hurt me and leave me. So, for years, no matter how hard she fought, I believed and held to the "truth" in my head that I couldn't let her get too close. I realize now that I met my match when I met her!

Kar'Michay Pope

She fought hard for my freedom, my joy, my life, and as much as I tried to keep her from doing it, she began to look behind the mask. Little did I know that my life was about to change... only this time it was for the better, and this time it would not be temporary.

I was very broken when I moved to Huntsville, Alabama. I was full of pain, anger, and confusion, and I did not know what to do with it. I thought keeping it somehow left me connected to the past that I seemed to not be able to let go of. One part of me wanted so desperately to be free, while the other part of me wanted to stay broken. I knew what broken felt like; I had felt that all my life. I did not know what freedom was like, nor did I want to be disappointed when freedom turned against me and failed me like everything else in life did. Trauma was my story and my identity, and I wanted to have something that was mine. I did not want to lose my identity or have it wrapped up in a false narrative. It seemed as if trauma followed me, and triumph was just a dream that I could not attain.

Somehow, God knew better than me and decided to walk with me through my pain to freedom. He was determined not to let me stay in bondage, He was determined not to let me stay broken, He was determined to convert my trauma to triumph. And despite how much I wanted to stay in my pit of despair, He was determined to pull me out of it. Do not think I did not fight against Him. I absolutely did. Getting to freedom was no easy task. I had to go through a lot of internal work... years of it. I did not give in to Him and His way without a fight. I was fighting against freedom because I did not really trust in

God to deliver me from the hurt and pain. Like most people who are going through healing, I wanted God to just take everything from me at once, for Him to come down from heaven and remove all that I was going through in my life. I mean, after all I'd been through, didn't I deserve that? I did not want to do the work that it would take to get better. I didn't even think I had the strength to do it anyway. If He was this big, all-knowing, all-powerful God, then I knew that if He wanted to, He could just come down and snap His fingers and make everything all better. Instead of Him doing all of that, what He did was give me the tools to fight. He gave me my parents to help walk with me through it every treacherous step of the way, and He gave me the strength to fight. Even with these tools, I needed His help to lead me and guide me through the journey because, little did I know, it would be a grueling one. Trust me, the healing process can be just as painful as the moment the abuse and trauma occurred.

After a while, I just gave in to His plan for me. I gave in to healing over pain, I gave in to peace over past hurts, and I gave in to love and forgiveness over holding onto anger. I honestly didn't think that God's way would work. I know that sounds crazy, but I just couldn't fathom that even God had a path to peace for me. Now I can say emphatically: never ever could I have imagined my life being what it is today. Never ever could I have imagined true freedom from my past, and never ever would I have believed that choosing life over death would be the choice that I would actually make on my own. I now live a life of freedom: freedom from my outside abuse and freedom from my inner pain. I live a life that is not filled with chaos and destruction, but with love and restoration. I still have my days when everything seems to not be going my way, when I want to run and hide, when I have to be careful not to react the way I used to. However, on those days, I find myself remembering where I came from and how far I have come, and I cannot help but rejoice amid it all. One thing that I have learned along this journey is that I am on a path to greatness, and I embrace it. I am literally living my best life, and it is truly up to me to go forth and do great things. With God's help, I accept the challenge!

Personal Discovery:

During this story, I once thought that my trauma defined me; that the pain I carried was a permanent part of who I was. But through deep reflection, healing, and the courage to confront what once broke me, I discovered that my scars were not signs of weakness but of survival. My journey from trauma to triumph has taught me that strength isn't the absence of struggle; it's rising in spite of it. Today, I stand not as a victim of my past but as proof that growth is possible, that wounds can become wisdom, and that even the darkest chapters can lead to the brightest victories.

1. Looking back on your moments of survival, what decision(s) are you most proud of?
2. What strengths have you discovered within yourself on your own journey from trauma to triumph?
3. What support systems do you currently have, and what support do you need for this journey?

4. What lessons from this journey will guide you in the future?

Therapeutic Ways to Release

Releasing pain and trauma in healthy ways is key to healing and regaining control over your life. While trauma can't always be "fixed" quickly, there are powerful and healthy outlets that help process and release emotional and physical pain over time. Below is a list of holistic, trauma-informed methods that are both accessible and supportive. **Important Notes:**

- **Trauma work should always be paced and grounded.** Safety and trust in the therapeutic relationship are essential.
- **It's okay to start small.** Even learning grounding exercises or understanding your triggers is part of healing.
- **A qualified trauma-informed therapist** can guide you toward techniques most appropriate for your unique history and needs.
- **There is no "right" pace.** Healing is non-linear; setbacks are part of the process.
- **Start with safety.** Only dive deeper when you feel secure and supported.
- **Celebrate progress.** Even getting out of bed can be a victory.

Emotional Expression

1. Talk to a Trusted Person
   - Whether it's a therapist, friend, or support group, sharing your story helps unburden you.

- Try not to bottle things up—what stays hidden tends to stay painful.

2. Journaling
- Write freely about your emotions, dreams, fears, or memories.
- Try techniques like "unsent letters" (to someone who hurt you, or even your younger self).

3. Crying
- It's not a breakdown—it's a release. Crying activates the parasympathetic nervous system and can bring emotional relief.

Body-Based and Mindfulness Techniques

1. Mindfulness and Meditation 1
- Encourages present-moment awareness and emotional regulation.
- Helps reduce anxiety and hypervigilance associated with trauma.

2. Yoga for Trauma (e.g., Trauma-Sensitive Yoga)
- Uses breath, gentle movement, and body awareness to restore safety in the body.
- Emphasizes choice and empowerment.

3. Breathwork
- Deep breathing techniques can help calm the nervous system and release held emotional energy.
- Box Breathing: In for 4 hold for 4 out for 4 hold for 4 etc…

Creative and Expressive Therapies

7. Art Therapy
- Helps express emotions nonverbally through drawing, painting, or sculpting.
- Especially helpful for those who struggle to talk about their trauma.

8. Music or Dance/Movement Therapy
- Uses rhythm and movement to express and process trauma.
- Can reconnect individuals to joy, spontaneity, and embodiment.

Mental & Emotional Practices

9. Self-Compassion
- Treat yourself as you would a loved one in pain.
- Practice saying things like: *"It's okay to feel this,"* or *"I'm doing the best I can."*

10. Mindfulness and Meditation 2
- Sit with your emotions without judgment. Notice them, name them, let them pass.
- Apps like Insight Timer or Headspace offer guided practices.

11. Visualization
- Imagine a safe space or light filling your body, gently washing away pain.
- Use this during flashbacks or overwhelming emotions.

Spiritual or Reflective Practices

12. Nature Connection
- Time in nature can be grounding and soothing.
- Even a short walk, watching the sky, or touching a tree can be healing.

13. Intentional Practices
- Light a candle to symbolize letting go.
- Write your pain down and safely burn or tear up the paper.
- Rituals offer symbolic release and closure.

www.ingramcontent.com/pod-product-compliance
Lightning Source LLC
Chambersburg PA
CBHW021626120626
46545CB00002B/426